D1346181

AN INTRODUCTION TO CANON LAW
IN THE CHURCH OF ENGLAND

AN INTRODUCTION TO
CANON LAW
IN THE
CHURCH OF ENGLAND

Being the Lichfield Cathedral
Divinity Lectures
for 1956

By

ERIC WALDRAM KEMP
B.D., M.A.

Fellow and Chaplain of Exeter College, Oxford,
and Canon and Prebendary of Caistor in Lincoln Cathedral

LONDON
HODDER AND STOUGHTON

First printed 1957

Printed in Great Britain
for Hodder and Stoughton Limited
by Richard Clay and Company, Ltd.,
Bungay, Suffolk

FOREWORD

By The Rt. Rev. J. W. C. Wand, K.C.V.O., P.C., D.D.

THE study of Canon Law has been too much neglected in the Church of England during recent generations. The reason, no doubt, is that we have been tied to the Canons of 1604, and the subject has therefore appeared to be exhausted. Since, however, the project for the revision of our Canons has been actively promoted in the Convocations and in the Assembly the whole matter has come alive and is now encouraging attention on every hand. If the project is to be carried through successfully, it is obvious that we must all be as well educated as possible in the principles of Canon Law. A mere pragmatic effort to meet our present needs without reference to the principles on which the whole science is based could only lead to disaster.

We could have no better guide to such a study than Canon Kemp, who is one of the foremost authorities in our Church on the subject. The opportunity to give some popular talks on it came to him through an invitation to fulfil the duties of the Divinity Lectureship at Lichfield Cathedral. This Lectureship is an ancient foundation, instituted in the time of Elizabeth I. It is a happy coincidence that, in the reign of the second Elizabeth, a topic which was of peculiar importance in the reign of the first should once more be revived.

The incidental and historical manner in which the author has dealt with the subject, while being of interest to the expert, should make this book an easy and delightful introduction for the beginner and for the general reader.

✠ WM: WAND

INTRODUCTION

WHEN, in November, 1955, the Dean and Chapter of Lichfield did me the honour to invite me to be their Divinity Lecturer for the following year, they expressed the hope that I would speak on "The Canon Law of the Church" in a general way, not confining myself to the present revision. In the three lectures which are printed here I have tried to sketch some of the background of the present revision of the canon law of the Church of England and to bring out certain points which the history of the subject suggests to me to be of particular importance.

The first lecture deals with the medieval canon law, because considerable parts of that are still the law of the Church of England, and because its highly developed system contained principles of jurisprudence which I believe to be of permanent value. This lecture necessarily compresses into a short space subjects which are still to some extent matters of historical controversy. It is my hope that the compression has not resulted in unfairness or inaccuracy.

The second lecture is devoted to the men who as judges and lawyers administered the law of the Church of England from the fourteenth century to the nineteenth, because it does not seem to me that a legal system can be properly understood apart from its context, and the men who administer the law are a most important part of that context. The Church of England is sometimes abused as being heavily clericalized, and it is forgotten what a very considerable part lay lawyers have played and continue to play in its history. In the last seventy or eighty years they have been much criticized, and with some reason as this lecture may indicate, but their services have been invaluable and deserve more recognition than they usually receive.

In the third lecture, on the basis of a number of cases found in manuscript and printed sources, some account is given of the maintenance of principles of the medieval jurisprudence in the reformed Church of England in the period before the great doctrinal and ritual trials of the last century. It is argued that for two hundred years after the Reformation the Church was in possession of a jurisprudence and a legal system which were inopportunely destroyed, but which if left to themselves might have moderated much of the controversial history of the last century. In conclusion some lessons for the present revision are drawn from the facts which have been set out.

I am deeply grateful for the honour and opportunity afforded by the invitation to give these lectures, and for the hospitality which I enjoyed at Lichfield. I am also grateful to many friends who allowed me to discuss various points with them and who guided me to books of which I should otherwise have been ignorant.

E. K.

June, 1956.

CONTENTS

REFERENCES

D.N.B.   *Dictionary of National Biography.*

Haggard   J. Haggard, *Reports of cases argued and determined in the Consistory Court of London containing the judgments of the Right Hon. Sir William Scott,* London (1882), 2 vols.

Lee   J. Phillimore, *Reports of cases argued and determined in the Arches and Prerogative Courts of Canterbury, and in the High Court of Delegates: containing the judgments of the Right Hon. Sir George Lee,* London (1833), 2 vols.

Phillimore   J. Phillimore, *Reports of cases argued and determined in the Ecclesiastical Courts at Doctors' Commons and in the High Court of Delegates,* London (1827), 3 vols.

I

THE subject of the authority possessed by the canon law in medieval England attracted the attention at the end of the last century of two of the greatest institutional historians that this country, and indeed one might say the world, has produced—William Stubbs and Frederic William Maitland. Dr Stubbs put forward his views first in Appendix I to the Report of the Royal Commission on the Ecclesiastical Courts in 1883, and then three years later in two chapters of his *Seventeen Lectures on the Study of Medieval and Modern History and kindred subjects.* From the fact that these two chapters are dated April, 1882, it may be inferred that they arose out of the work which he did for the Royal Commission. Stubbs was a man of immense learning and breadth of view, and his historical work proper is marked by a strong element of caution. Professor J. G. Edwards has pointed out that this was not, in Stubbs' case, mere hedging, and he has quoted a remark of his that "History knows that it can wait for more evidence and review its older verdicts; it offers an endless series of courts of appeal, and is ever ready to re-open closed cases." [1] It is important to bear this in mind in considering his theory about the canon law in England.

In his Appendix to the Royal Commission's Report Stubbs wrote: "The laws of the Church of England from the Conquest onwards, were, as before, the customary church law developed by the legal and scientific ability of its administrators, and occasionally improved and added to by the con-

[1] J. G. Edwards, *William Stubbs*, London 1952 (Historical Association Pamphlet), p. 7.

stitutions of successive archbishops, the canons of national councils, and the sentences, or authoritative answers to questions, propounded by the Popes." A little further on he said:

The laws which guided the English courts up to the time of the Reformation may then be thus arranged:—

1. The canon law of Rome, comprising the decretum of Gratian, the decretals of Gregory IX. published in 1230, the Sext, added by Boniface VIII., the Clementines issued in 1318, and the Extravagants or uncodified edicts of the succeeding Popes.

A knowledge of these was the scientific equipment of the ecclesiastical jurist, but the texts were not authoritative. The English barons and the king at the Council of Merton refused to allow the national law of marriage to be modified by them, and it was held that they were of no force at all when and where they were opposed to the laws of England.

2. The civil law of Rome was, so far as procedure went, an important part of legal education, but this, from the reign of Stephen onwards, was refused any recognition except as a scientific authority in England, was kept under even more jealous restrictions than the canon law, and was only tolerated in those departments of law, such as the maritime and matrimonial, for which the national law afforded no adequate directions, and in which it was especially important that English practice should agree with that of foreign nations.

3. The provincial law of the Church of England contained, as has been stated, the constitutions of the archbishops from Langton downwards, and the canons passed in the legatine councils under Otho and Othobon. The latter, which might possibly be treated as in themselves wanting the sanction of the national church, were ratified in councils held by Peckham. The commentaries of John of Ayton and the carefully edited digest of Bishop Lyndwood were the finally received texts of this portion of the law, and contained large extracts from the civil and canon law of Rome; but the comments were not . . .

received as equal in authority to statute law. The provincial constitutions of Canterbury were received in York in 1462.[1]

It would be reasonable to conclude that Stubbs believed that the Roman canon law, as contained particularly in the *Corpus Juris Canonici* and proceeding in the main from the popes, did not or was not regarded as possessing any inherent authority in England, other than as a useful and scientific guide. The text of the Report seems to sum up the position in a sentence when it says: "But the canon law of Rome, though always regarded as of great authority in England, was not held to be binding on the courts." [2] This view was directly challenged by Maitland.

Maitland [3] pointed out that the provincial legislation of the English Church presupposed the existence and authority of the Roman canon law. If we were to go by Lyndwood's *Provinciale* alone, for example, we should have to say that the medieval English Church had hardly any marriage law at all, for Lyndwood's Book IV, dealing with marriage, contains only four chapters. The 166 chapters in the Decretals of Gregory IX and those which are to be found in other parts of the Corpus are assumed. But one can go beyond this and point to the explicit statements of the medieval canonists, of whom William Lyndwood, Dean of the Arches, Prolocutor of Convocation, Keeper of the Privy Seal, Bishop of St David's, is the principal witness. He says bluntly that no archbishop can repeal the decrees of a papal legate: *et verum est, quod constitutiones legatinas non poterit archiepiscopus tollere, quia inferior non potest tollere legem superioris.*[4] This makes short work of any view that the constitutions of the legates Otho

[1] *Report of the Commissioners appointed to inquire into the Constitution and Working of the Ecclesiastical Courts*, London, 1883, i, p. 25.
[2] Ibid. i, p. xviii.
[3] F. W. Maitland, *Roman Canon Law in the Church of England*, London, 1898, chapters 1–3.
[4] W. Lyndwood, *Provinciale*, Oxford, 1679, p. 154, gl. ad v. *Adjiciendo.*

and Othobon needed the sanction of archbishop Pecham. Again Lyndwood says that archbishops may add to the constitutions of the Roman pontiffs, provided that the substance is preserved: *maxime cum archiepiscopi possint ad constitutiones Romanorum pontificum addere, salva ipsarum substantia.*[1] And further, "It may happen that someone violates the canons believing that the Roman Church has no power of making canons; and such an one will be punished as a heretic." *Potest tamen esse quod aliquis violet canones, credens quod ecclesia Romana non habet potestatem canones condendi: et talis punitur ut haereticus.*[2]

These quotations will perhaps suffice to make the point, and there is no need to labour it, for the view that the pope's authority was regarded as binding, at least in theory, in medieval England is now accepted by virtually all medieval historians, and one might add by the lawyers when they are not being lawyers. But perhaps even as lawyers, in view of the well-known touchiness of the English Common Law on the subject of private property, they might be impressed by the apparently unanimous opinion of the judges given in the reign of King Edward IV that "the Pope can write to the Bishop of Canterbury and compel him to summon his clergy to grant an aid to defend the Faith" and that the King cannot exempt anyone from paying aid to the Pope.[3]

Now Dr Stubbs had the highest respect for the work of Professor Maitland, and in the later editions of his lectures he made some interesting modifications of his text in view of Maitland's criticisms. He also added some footnotes and two pages of introduction. In the introduction he said that he was conscious of having over-stated his views and that the lectures were susceptible of a good deal of correction and criticism,

[1] Op. cit. p. 137, gl. ad v. *Innodatus.*
[2] Ibid. p. 38, gl. ad v. *Reluctantes.*
[3] M. Hemmant, *Select Cases in the Exchequer Chamber* (Selden Society), ii, p. 11.

and he referred his readers explicitly to Maitland's book saying: "I have so great respect for his knowledge, critical insight, and fairness, that I would gladly submit to any amount of adjustment of facts and authorities that he might prescribe to me." But Stubbs continued with this paragraph.

There is however a discrepancy between his general conclusions on the authority which the Canon Law of Rome had in England before the Reformation and the theory which is more than once stated by me in these lectures and elsewhere. The one view concludes that the Canon Law of Rome as held in England was regarded not only with respect but as absolutely binding. The other, which is more or less the opinion that has been held by English jurists, is that the authority given to the Corpus Juris Canonici in practice was rather of the nature of scientific jurisprudence than of recognized, accepted and enacted law. . . .

I have thought and intended to maintain my belief that the Corpus Juris Canonici in its various expansions affected the law and process of the English courts, which had been framed before the Decretum was published, not as statute law, but rather as case law, or precedents, or as in a sense modifying or expounding the common law of the Church; determining the mind of the judge rather than pronouncing indisputable or immediately applicable conclusions. In this I may have been quite wrong: if so I would have these lectures read with that amount and measure of reserve. On the other hand I never doubted that within its own area of applicability the Roman Canon Law did practically govern the ecclesiastical courts wherever it was not contrariant to the common law, nor overruled by the use of prohibitions, or thrown out of use by the protests of parliaments or such statutes as those of Praemunire and Provisors. That a code liable to be overruled in such ways should be regarded as having a vitality and force analogous to that of the national law in temporal matters—that is, that the Corpus Juris stood, in the strict ecclesiastical courts, on the same level as the Statute Book in the temporal courts, I could not see; and knowing that what authority it had it owed rather to tacit assumption than to formal and constitutional acceptance by Church or State, I offered my explanation as sufficient. The question does not affect the fact, but the nature of the authority.[1]

This paragraph may be set side by side with the following two sentences from Maitland:

> But if we turn to the three collections of decretals that were issued by Gregory IX., Boniface VIII., and John XXII., there can surely be no doubt as to the character that they were meant to bear by those who issued them, or as to the character that they bore in the eyes of those who commented upon them. Each of them was a statute book deriving its force from the pope who published it, and who, being pope, was competent to ordain binding statutes for the catholic church and every part thereof, at all events within those spacious limits that were set even to papal power by the *ius divinum et naturale*.[2]

Subsequent writers have, it seems to me, tended rather to treat the difference of opinion between Stubbs and Maitland as if it were a difference about the English recognition of papal authority in the Middle Ages, and I would like to suggest that insufficient attention has been paid to the nature of the medieval canon law, which explains in part the difference of approach of these two great scholars. I propose now, therefore, to turn to that subject.

We must begin with some words about the contents of the *Corpus Juris Canonici*, and indeed perhaps the title itself should first be explained. During the Middle Ages it was used at different times to apply to different things. In the middle of the thirteenth century it was used of the *Decretum Gratiani*, at other times it was given to the five so-called *Compilationes antiquae*. Most commonly it came to be ap-

---

[1] W. Stubbs, *Seventeen Lectures on the Study of Medieval and Modern History and kindred subjects*, Oxford, 3rd edn. (1900), pp. 335 f. cf. L. T. Dibdin, *Roman Canon Law in England*, Quarterly Review, ccxvii (1912), pp. 413–36.

[2] Maitland, op. cit. p. 3.

plied to the three big official collections of papal decretals made in the thirteenth and fourteenth centuries. Between 1499 and 1502 the two French canonists Jean Chappuis and Vitalis de Thèbes published in three folio volumes the *Decretum Gratiani*, the three official collections of papal decretals, and two small collections of decretals which had been issued at a later date and which they called the *Extravagantes Joannis XXII* and the *Extravagantes communes*. Pope Gregory XIII (1572–85) in the bull *Cum munere* gave a quasi-official recognition to the use of the term *Corpus Juris Canonici* as it was applied to these six books. This piece of bibliographical history may put us on our guard against using this comparatively modern term unreservedly in medieval circumstances. Let us, however, look at the component parts of the *Corpus* a little more closely.

The *Decretum Gratiani*, which is the oldest and largest section, was put together about the year 1140 by one Master Gratian, who, apart from his book, is virtually unknown, but was a teacher of law in the University of Bologna. The *Decretum* consists of three parts of unequal length. The first is divided into 101 *Distinctiones*, each of which deals with a particular subject and puts together rules and decisions bearing on that subject drawn from all ages of the Church. The second part consists of thirty-six *Causae* which are the discussion of a miscellany of practical problems in the life of the Church in the twelfth century. Here Gratian's method is to divide each case into a number of *quaestiones* and then to argue out each question, bringing in canons, decretals, and the like for and against particular solutions. The third part, which is much shorter than the other two, is constructed on the same principles as the first. It contains five *Distinctiones*, which deal with the Dedication and Consecration of churches, the Eucharist, the Calendar and observance of feasts, Baptism, and Confirmation.

The second part of the *Corpus* is known as the Decretals

of Gregory IX. This collection was issued in 1234, and it consists chiefly of extracts from papal letters together with some canons of councils, notably of the fourth Lateran Council of 1215. This is an official collection, which Gratian's work was not, and the whole has the authority of Pope Gregory in addition to the authority already possessed by its component parts. It was followed in 1298 by the *Liber Sextus* of Boniface VIII, so called because the Decretals of Gregory were divided into five books and this new collection was issued as a supplement or sixth book. It also consists chiefly of papal decretals, but has also the canons of the two Councils of Lyons, and it, too, is an official collection. In 1317 the *Constitutiones Clementinae* were published by John XXII, having been originally collected by his predecessor Clement V. They contain more papal decretals and the canons of the Council of Vienne, and are an official collection. The origin of the two remaining parts of the *Corpus*, the two collections of *Extravagantes*, I have already described. They also consisted of papal decretals, but as collections were the work of private individuals, not of popes.

There can be little doubt that the work of making these collections and the title of *Corpus Juris* given to various of them was inspired by the example of the *Corpus Juris Civilis*, but there could hardly be a greater contrast between the two. The name *Corpus Juris Civilis* came from the twelfth century onwards to be applied in the West to the four books which contain the legislative work of the Emperor Justinian. They are first the Code. This, originally issued in 529, now survives only in the second edition of 534. It is based principally upon the older imperial codes, particularly the *Codex Theodosianus*, and has some changes, corrections, and additions to the old legislation made by Justinian himself. Secondly comes the Digest or Pandects, issued in 533, a collection of extracts from the most famous Roman lawyers codifying as it were the current jurisprudence. Third is the

Institutes, designed as an introduction to the first principles of law. In the letter to the Universities of Beyrouth and Constantinople the emperor decreed that the Institutes should be the basis of the first year of the study of law, the Digest should occupy the second, third, and fourth years, and the Code the fifth year. Finally in the *Corpus Juris Civilis* we have the Novels which are constitutions of Justinian published after the second edition of the Code and privately collected. The contrast between this complete and coherent *Corpus* as it appeared in the twelfth and thirteenth centuries and the incipient *Corpus Juris Canonici* is marked. It is also understandable that the canonists, studying side by side with the civil lawyers should have been greatly influenced by the *Corpus Juris Civilis* and have drawn greatly on it, particularly for the procedure of their courts. Of that there is more to be said later.

I hope that this description of the composition of the *Corpus Juris Canonici* and the comparison of it with the *Corpus Juris Civilis* may have done something already to raise in your minds questions about Maitland's use of the term "statute book". We must, however, remember that he excludes from this the *Decretum Gratiani* and applies it specifically to the three official collections of decretals. Each of these was, he says, "a statute book deriving its force from the pope who published it, and who, being pope, was competent to ordain binding statutes for the catholic church and every part thereof".

With this in mind I would ask you to look at chapter 6 of Book I, title ii of the Decretals of Gregory IX. This particular title is headed *De constitutionibus* and chapter 6 is part of a letter addressed by pope Innocent III in 1198 to the archbishop of Sens and the bishop of Troyes. In it he says that it had come to his notice that the canons of the cathedral of Troyes had made an order varying the apportionment of the chapter's revenue. Hitherto the common fund had been divided among all whether they were resident or absent, now any canons appointed after the date of this constitution were to receive their portion only when they were resident. Further, there were vines the produce of which had been annexed to individual prebends, and the new constitution decreed that as the canons died the vines should not become the property of their successors, but the produce should be divided among the whole chapter. The pope attacks this new constitution on the grounds that it introduces an inequality between the old and the new canons and lays down the principle that he who makes a law for another should be prepared to obey it himself. He orders the archbishop and the bishop to restore equality among the canons either on the basis of the constitution observed down to the time of the making of the new one or according to some reasonable rule.

One may well ask whether this is the sort of thing that one expects to find in a statute book, and yet things of this kind form a very large part of the collections of decretals and they were embodied for the sake of the general principles which the compilers saw in them. In this particular instance the principle is that a constitution which is for the benefit of certain members of a college and to the detriment of others ought not to hold good without a reasonable cause. It is true of course that in the Decretals there are certain things which we might more properly call statutes. There is, for example, chapter 12 of title 38, Book V of the Decretals of Gregory IX, which is canon 21 of the fourth Lateran Council (1215), ordering all christians who have reached years of discretion to confess their sins to their own parish priest once every year at Easter. There is also chapter 42 of title 6 of Book I, which is canon 23 of the same council and lays down the three canonical methods of election—scrutiny, compromission, and inspiration. The great bulk of the chapters of the Decretals are, however, papal decisions and directions given in particular cases which were brought to the pope on appeal or answers to bishops who submitted cases for the papal ruling.[1] These are more akin to what we should call precedents, and if we are to give a modern title to the Decretals a more accurate one than that of statute book would be "Leading cases in the canon law".

This being so, very great scope was left to the glossator and commentator, and for the student of the medieval canon law it is almost as important to know what the gloss and the writings of the great commentators say as what the text of the *Corpus* says. Each of the great collections of decretals was glossed within a comparatively short time of its publication. The gloss is a brief commentary written in the margin and round the actual text, and for each collection there was one gloss which became generally accepted and is known as the *glossa ordinaria*. The *glossa ordinaria* to the Decretals of Gregory IX was composed in four stages by Bernard of Parma, who died in 1266, on the basis of existing glosses to some of the earlier collections.[2] Those to the Sext and the Clementines were written by Joannes Andreae, one of the most famous of the Bolognese canonists, and incidentally a married layman with a large family.[3]

A rather startling example of the importance of the commentators is to be found in the medieval teaching about the enforcement of contracts.[4] The principle of the Roman civil law was that a contract could not be enforced by an action at law unless it was couched in the proper legal forms, a *pactum*

[1] For a convenient collection of some of these decretals in their original form see W. Holtzmann and E. W. Kemp, *Papal Decretals relating to the Diocese of Lincoln in the twelfth century*, Lincoln Record Society, vol. 47 (1954).

[2] S. Kuttner and B. Smalley, "The 'Glossa Ordinaria' to the Gregorian Decretals," *English Historical Review*, lx (1945).

[3] J. F. von Schulte, *Die Geschichte der Quellen und Literatur des Canonischen Rechts von Papst Gregor IX. bis zum Concil von Trient*, Stuttgart (1877), ii, pp. 205–29.

[4] For the next four paragraphs see F. Spies, *De l'observation des simples conventions en droit canonique*, Paris (1928).

vestitum. A simple promise, referred to sometimes as a *nudum pactum*, would not do. The canonists, with their great emphasis upon morality, taught emphatically that promises ought to be kept, but they differed among themselves for some time about the question of enforcement. Some, of whom the most prominent was pope Innocent IV, author of a commentary on the decretals in the middle of the thirteenth century, did not allow that a proper legal action could arise from a *nudum pactum*. He held that the only way of dealing with a man who refused to carry out an agreement which rested on a simple promise was that laid down in the Gospel according to St Matthew 18. 15–17, and generally referred to as the *denunciatio evangelica*. This required four stages, first personal rebuke, then rebuke before witnesses, then complaint to the church, and finally, if the offender proved obdurate, excommunication. The aim of the whole process was penal and remedial. It was concerned primarily with the moral state of the offender and only secondarily with any question of reparation for the damage resulting from his failure to carry out his promise.

A contemporary canonist, Joannes Teutonicus, who died 1245/46, took a very different view. He found in one of the *Causae* in the *Decretum* of Gratian a passage from St John Chrysostom to the effect that the Lord wishes there to be no difference between our oaths and our speech, so that as there should be no perjury in regard of our oaths so there should be no lying in regard of our speech. The whole passage is based upon our Lord's teaching about oaths in the Sermon on the Mount. Joannes Teutonicus takes speech as equivalent to promises and deduces that no distinction is to be made between full-dress oaths or contracts and simple promises, and that therefore *ex nudo pacto oritur actio*. The great thirteenth-century canonist Hostiensis takes a similar view, but bases it rather on grounds of equity. They were followed by most of the leading canonists of the fourteenth century. Guido de Baisio, who died in 1313, has an interesting comment on the difference between the civil and canon laws on this point when he says that the motive of the difference is *canonica aequitas* and that the canon law tends to apply equity in relations between individuals and does not occupy itself with the subtleties of the civil law. By the end of the fourteenth century the view that an action arises from a *nudum pactum* has become the *communis opinio canonistarum*, though its full application is held to be restricted to clerks and to laymen who are under the temporal jurisdiction of the church.

In the fifteenth century Cardinal Zabarella attacked this view, maintaining that the civil law ought to be followed unless the canon law expressly derogated from it, and arguing that in this case the canonical texts had been misinterpreted. John of Imola (died 1436) inclines towards Innocent IV and Zabarella, but he recognizes that the opposite view is the *communis opinio* and that it will be followed by the courts. The *communis opinio* is followed by the leading canonist of the fifteenth century, Nicholas de Tudeschis. A canonist of the turn of the fourteenth and fifteenth centuries, Anthony de Butrio (1338–1408), has an interesting comment. He observes that in the civil law if a *nudum pactum* has been confirmed by law, then an action does arise, and he argues that every *nudum pactum* is in fact confirmed by the natural law that men ought to keep their promises and that this is a divine law. In consequence the canon law grants an action in support of these promises. The difference is to be explained by the different ends pursued by the two laws: *Dico quod ideo, quia ius civile principaliter non insequiter finem iuris divini sed finem publicae utilitatis.*

Now one may very well ask what relation all this argument has to the text of the *Corpus*, what legal basis is to be found there for the view which finally prevailed. One of the texts used I have already quoted and there are six others which figure prominently in the discussions. Three of them are from the *Decretum*. They are a letter from pope Gregory I in which he says that he is going to perform a promise which he had made to the predecessor of a certain bishop; a canon of the fourth council of Toledo (A.D. 633) ordering a bishop to pay what he had promised to a workman; and a letter of pope Nicholas I (858–67) insisting on the voluntary element in marriage. The remaining three are from the Decretals of Gregory IX. Here we have a canon of the Council of Carthage *c.* 348 ordering two bishops to observe an agreement which they had made about the boundaries of their dioceses; another letter of Gregory I saying that people ought to try to perform what they have promised; and a letter of pope Lucius III (1181–4) ordering the bishop of Ely and the archdeacon of Norwich to inquire into the case of a clerk who had gone surety for some of the London clergy and they had defaulted so that he had had to pay up. The bishop and the archdeacon are required to see that he is reimbursed by the original debtors. It is obvious that none of these texts clearly supports either view in this branch of the law, and that, I hope, illustrates sufficiently the importance of the canon law teachers in building up a body of law in the Middle Ages. I hope that it also illustrates the extent to which in doing so they were moved by the desire to give practical effect to the principles of the Gospel.

The next subjects about which something must be said are custom and dispensation, but we must glance briefly at the medieval theory of law as it is set out at the beginning of the *Decretum*. Gratian starts with the famous sentence: *Humanum genus duobus regitur naturali videlicet iure et moribus* (the human race is governed by two things namely natural law and customs). The natural law is that which is common to all nations and is based upon natural instinct. It is contained in the Law and in the Gospel by which one is ordered to do to others as one would be done by and forbidden to do what one

24

would not wish to be done to oneself. Ignorance of the natural law is always to be condemned in those of mature years and no dispensation from it can be accepted save when a man is compelled to choose between two evils. The natural law is often formulated and applied by human law, and human laws which are contrary to it are unjust and must be rejected. All human law, Gratian holds, is properly speaking a form of custom: a written law is instituted by promulgation but is conformed by the custom of those who use it and abrogated by their disuse of it.

The canon law partly expresses natural law and Scripture, and in that is immutable, but it is largely human law made by ecclesiastical authority and mutable. In the normal way the canons which are rules made by the proper authorities in the church are binding on all members of the church and to refuse to obey them is to refuse the authority of God, from whom this legislative power comes.

Written law in the church, however, was regarded as subject to two forms of modification—dispensation and custom. Canons exist, it was held, for particular reasons, and when those reasons do not operate the canon should be declared suspended. Ivo, bishop of Chartres at the beginning of the twelfth century, wrote that the greater part of the canon law was made up of precepts of the church which were only means for securing the salvation of souls and, as means, of varying value. He taught that it was not sufficient that a law should be just, it must harmonize with the age and country in which it was applied, and if it ceased to do so authority should dispense from its observance. Dispensations, however, ought only to be given for grave reasons but might be for private as well as public considerations. The right of dispensation belonged to all ecclesiastical superiors who used it under the control of the pope.[1] Dispensations

[1] P. Fournier, *Yves de Chartres et le droit canonique*, Revue des Questions historiques, lxiii (1890), pp. 51 f. and pp. 384 f. On the

were widely used in the Middle Ages, in particular in the fields of marriage, pluralities, and residence.

St Thomas Aquinas says that custom [1] is the expression in act of the human will enlightened by reason just as law is the expression in writing of the same will. The contemporary canonist Hostiensis describes custom as "a reasonable use, prescribed and established for a suitable time, uninterrupted by any contrary act, brought in by two actions or a judgment or before the limit of memory, and approved by general usage". The operation of custom is five-fold. It imitates law, supplying deficiencies, it interprets law when a doubt is raised, it abrogates law, it derogates from existing law, it creates a presumption. We may know that custom to be reasonable which is approved by law, observed and ordered by the Roman Church. Generally we may know a custom to be unreasonable which is expressly attacked by law, or is in other ways evil, e.g. if it is contrary to the natural law or to the decrees of a council touching matters of faith. As regards the length of time necessary to establish a custom, Hostiensis says that some canonists require *longa consuetudo*, others *longaeva*. *Longa* is ten or twenty years, but for a custom to acquire the force of a prescription it must have forty years' uninterrupted use.

Joannes Andreae at the end of the thirteenth century defines custom as "a kind of law instituted by the usage of those who by public authority are able to make law", and he says that three conditions are necessary: 1. frequency of acts; 2. consent of a majority of the people; 3. a certain length of time to make clear the intention of those who practise the

---

general subject of dispensations see J. Brys, *De dispensatione in iure canonico*, Bruges (1925), and *Dispensation in Practice and Theory*, the Report of a Commission appointed by the Archbishop of Canterbury, London (1944).

[1] On the subject of custom see R. Wehrlé, *De la coutume dans le droit canonique*, Paris (1928).

custom. The canonists, he says, admit ten years for a custom which is *praeter legem* but require forty for one *contra legem*. This definition was criticized in the fifteenth century by Nicholas de Tudeschis on the grounds that it might be understood as allowing a custom introduced against the canons by the inferiors of a pope. He insists that custom draws its force not only from the tacit consent of ecclesiastics but also from the authority of the pope who allows a custom contrary to the canons to be introduced—in other words, the consent of the sovereign is necessary to give the force of law to custom. Theory and practice, however, are both reconciled and saved by saying that the consent may be tacit.

Now it can be shown that in several ways the operation of the general canon law was modified in England by custom. One sphere was that of ritual. A constitution of archbishop Chichele ordered the observance throughout the province of Canterbury of the feast of St John of Beverley *secundum usum Saresbiriensis ecclesiae*. Lyndwood commenting on this says that it is opposed to a text in the Decretum which lays down that in every province the use of the metropolitical church is to be the norm. But, he says, in England, the use of Salisbury is the norm *ex longa consuetudine*.[1] Another sphere was that of patronage. From the time of King Henry II the royal courts in England more and more took control of cases involving rights of patronage of ecclesiastical benefices and this was recognized to a considerable extent by a constitution of archbishop Boniface. Lyndwood, commenting on this in two places, accepts this as a matter of custom. Commenting on the words *Foro Regio* he says: "In which a case of the law of patronage is treated by custom of the realm of England, although according to the canons it belongs to the ecclesiastical court".[2] In the other place, commenting on the expression *Jure Patronatus*, he says: "Whose cognizance the

[1] Lyndwood, op. cit. p. 104, gl. ad v. *Usum Sarum Ecclesiae.*
[2] Ibid. p. 217.

27

King's court claims to belong to itself, although the case of the right of patronage may be annexed to spirituals and thus belong to the ecclesiastical court. But custom gives cognizance to the temporal court, and this seems to be recognized by this constitution in this place." [1] A third point which still affects us to-day is that whereas the general canon law made the rector of a church responsible for the repair of the whole, custom in England limited his responsibility to the chancel and assigned the nave to the parishioners. [2]

Another field in which we may perhaps see the operation of custom is that of clerical taxation. The third Lateran council of 1179 decreed that laymen who imposed taxes on clerks or churches were to be excommunicated, but allowed that a bishop and his clergy might grant a subsidy in case of great need. The fourth Lateran council in 1215 tightened this permission by requiring that the pope's consent be obtained. In 1296 this requirement was confirmed by Pope Boniface VIII in the bull *Clericis laicos*. All these three texts are to be found in the Decretal collections and were the subject of comment by the canonists. They discussed at length whether in certain circumstances the clergy could be regarded as morally bound to contribute to the expenses of the defence and government of a country. The early fifteenth-century canonist Petrus de Ancharano, himself a layman, clearly thought that the clergy ought to share in the common burden of taxation for the defence of a town or country and for the maintenance of public works such as fortifications and breakwaters. He argued that as clerks and laymen enjoyed the same benefits it was only reasonable that both should contribute to the cost. He, however, like other canonists, felt himself constrained by the uncompromising words of the papal prohibitions which, at the end of the thirteenth cen-

[1] Lyndwood, op. cit. p. 316.
[2] Ibid. p. 250 gl. ad v. *Defectus Ecclesiae*; p. 253 gl. ad v. *Navis Ecclesiae*.

tury, had produced violent conflicts between king and clergy in both France and England. He remarks that he has been told by a trustworthy person that in England the churches are required to bear a fourth part of the burdens which are imposed generally for the necessities of the realm, but he adds that this composition cannot be based on law if the pope has not been consulted. If we look at some of the figures which have been published concerning the revenues of the Crown in the fifteenth century, we shall see that the man who gave Petrus de Ancharano his information was not very wide of the mark. Mr Kirby tells us that on an average over the years 1413–16 a parliamentary grant of a fifteenth produced £36,000 and a clerical grant of a tenth £15,000. That brings the total revenue from direct taxation to £51,000, of which the clergy contributed rather more than a quarter. For reasons which do not concern us here the yield of a clerical grant dropped somewhat in the course of the century, but it is clear that throughout the whole of the fifteenth century taxation of ecclesiastical incomes was regarded by the government as a regular and normal source of revenue and was accepted as such by the leaders of the Church, who were themselves frequently great ministers of state, while their subordinates were drawn to a large extent from what we should call the civil service. There is no evidence that these contributions received papal authority in any other way than by silence, but they were a most important feature in the life of the English Church and a principal factor influencing the survival and constitution of the Convocations, and in particular the extensive powers possessed by the Lower Houses. And all this was a matter of custom which drastically modified the application of the texts of the law.[1]

[1] See E. W. Kemp, "The Origins of the Canterbury Convocation," *Journal of Ecclesiastical History*, iii (1952), pp. 132–43. For the financial details see J. L. Kirby, "The issues of the Lancastrian exchequer and Lord Cromwell's estimates of 1433," *Bulletin of the*

I hope that what has been said in this lecture has conveyed some idea of the complex nature of the old canon law which lies behind our own modern enactments and still forms part of the law of our church. In the third lecture we shall see how it was used and applied in the English courts after the Reformation, but in the conclusion of this lecture I will refer to some comments on it made in the Report of the Canon Law Commission. The Commissioners contrasted the law of the Church with the Common Law of England and they said:

These three codes gave to the law of the Church in the middle ages a certain specific character. It was a law based on a code, as distinct from the Common Law of England, which is case law. The law of the Church knew nothing of the Common Law doctrine of binding precedents; the law was deduced from the three official codes; and in the rare cases when they contained no law applicable to the matter in hand, from the *Decretum* and the Roman Civil Law. But the actual form in which the law was couched lacks the scientific precision which a modern lawyer would demand from a code. The decretals had been issued in answer to questions of law addressed to the pope; but when they were included in codes and given the status of law throughout the whole Church, they were often so abbreviated as to become in many cases unintelligible. This difficulty has now been to a great extent removed, since, in their modern editions, Richter and Friedberg have inserted passages that were omitted from the original text of the *Corpus*. But in the middle ages it needed a number of great canonists, by their commentaries on the code, to make many of its chapters intelligible. A modern judge given the task of applying the bare text of a chapter as it is found in the official text of one of the codes would find much to criticize in the way of drafting and

Institute of Historical Research, xxiv (1951), p. 137 n. 2. For some further examples of liturgical custom which evaded the strict letter of the law see E. W. Kemp, *Canonization and Authority in the Western Church* (1948), chapter vi.

arrangement. Although the arrangement of the three codes was simpler and more convenient than that of the *Decretum*, it still was extraordinarily cumbersome and obscure; and, even to people trained to use it from their youth, finding a particular text must at times have been a long business. Even if much of the contents of these codes had not been covered by subsequent legislation in both the Church of Rome and the Church of England, yet their drafting and method of arrangement would make their use in their present form virtually impossible to-day. The middle ages created a great legal system for the Church; but it is quite wrong to idealize the system and to suppose that the Church is incapable of producing anything better. Legal science has advanced since the middle ages, and in no direction more than that of arrangement and drafting, there-by exposing the weaknesses of the Canon Law.[1]

With much of this I imagine that every student of the medieval canon law would agree. Government of all kinds was a cumbrous and inefficient business in the Middle Ages. And yet it seems to me that part at least of the complexity of the medieval canon law results from an endeavour to combine the application of high moral principles derived from the divine law with the greatest possible allowance for the freedom and individual development of the multitude of communities which made up the church. The first of these points we have seen in our glance at the canonical teaching about the en-forcement of contracts, the second is patent in the wide scope allowed to the operation of custom. The Western church as a whole was made up of a number of large communities which corresponded roughly to the national or regional churches, most of which had their own peculiarities and their own adaptations of the *ius commune*. Within our own regional church, the *Ecclesia Anglicana*, there were the com-munities of the two distinct provinces of Canterbury and

[1] *The Canon Law of the Church of England, Being the Report of the Archbishops' Commission on Canon Law, together with Proposals for a Revised Body of Canons* (1947), p. 35. (S.P.C.K.)

York, whose organization and outlook present very interesting contrasts. There were the communities of the various dioceses, the communities of the various individual or groups of religious houses, the community of the cathedral, and within each cathedral lesser communities of the chapter, the vicars choral, and so forth. Each parish formed a community and might have its own customs in the matter of tithes, or even to some extent of liturgical observance. Once one penetrates below the surface of medieval theory one always finds the greatest variety of practice, and in a sense this is an expression of the catholicity of the church, which is the church for all men, with their great diversities of temperament, education, and mental ability. The system of the medieval church in some ways produced anarchy, but it endeavoured to avoid tyranny so long as the fundamentals of the faith were not threatened. Its emphasis on moral principle combined with its respect for custom remind us of fundamental purposes of law which the modern desire for tidiness, efficiency, and uniformity may easily make us forget. There is something to be said for a complex and flexible system of jurisprudence, which will direct and educate, rather than a detailed written code which may easily strangle the christian life.

II

In our popular history books we hear much about the peculiar excellencies of the English Common Law and the unhappy plight of the inhabitants of those countries whose legal system is based upon the civil law of Rome. We may even be told how in the twelfth century an attempt was made to bring the civil law to this country and that it was sharply suppressed by the English king. It may therefore come as something of a surprise to find that when in 1399 most of the leading men of the country, both clerical and lay, had decided that they must somehow get rid of King Richard II and substitute a monarch who would have more respect for the rights of private property, they turned to the doctors of the canon and civil laws for a way in which to bring this about. For this piece of information we are indebted particularly to a member of the commission set up to advise on this point—Master Adam of Usk, a native of that Monmouthshire town, who was born about 1352 and died in 1430.[1]

Adam was doctor of laws, i.e. of civil and canon law, at Oxford and a papal notary. During the 1380s he taught the civil law at Oxford. From 1392 to 1399 he practised as an advocate in the ecclesiastical courts, and in addition to these occupations he held livings successively in Monmouthshire, Somerset, and Wiltshire, and also in plurality other livings in Essex, Monmouthshire, and Kent, with perhaps some other ecclesiastical posts. His part in the deposition of Richard II has just been mentioned. In the first year of the new reign

---

[1] On Adam of Usk see E. M. Thompson, *Chronicon Adae de Usk A.D. 1377–1421*, London (1904).

we find him appointed one of a commission to hear an appeal from a judgement of the military court of Bordeaux, and a little later "called on for an opinion on the question of the reimbursement to France of the portion of the dower of Richard's young widow, queen Isabella, which was repayable in default of issue of the marriage, and which Henry would have been glad to find some excuse for withholding".[1] At the same time he appears as counsel in various actions in the court of chivalry. He also seems to have been involved in the negotiations for the marriage of Henry IV's daughter Blanche to the son of the emperor and was certainly a member of convocation. About the same time he was commissioned by archbishop Arundel to investigate a scandal in the priory of Nuneaton.

Sad to relate, this distinguished man had to leave the country under a cloud in 1402. He had stolen a horse and been convicted as a common thief. On leaving England he made straight for the papal court, where he was very soon appointed papal chaplain and auditor, that is a judge of cases which came to the pope. He remained with the curia, sharing its vicissitudes, for about four years and then decided to return home. At first however he only reached Bruges, for, having arrived there, he was warned that he was still not *persona grata* in England and would be wise to wait for a royal pardon. He therefore stayed in Bruges for two years and apparently found no difficulty in making a living out of legal practice in Flanders. It was not until 1411 that he eventually returned to England and archbishop Arundel restored him to his practice in the court of Canterbury and in 1415 he reappears in convocation. After that he seems gradually to have dropped out of affairs.

Adam of Usk's career may seem remarkably assorted. We have a lawyer and a cleric, and he exercises his two professions in the ecclesiastical courts, in the court of chivalry, in

[1] E. M. Thompson, op. cit. p. xviii.

34

matters of international law and in matters of constitutional law, as well as taking an active part in convocation. This combination of activities, however, was not unusual. A little later in the fifteenth century we have Thomas Beckington.[1] He also was a doctor of civil law of Oxford, a New College man. In 1423 he appears as Dean of the Arches and ten years later is prolocutor of convocation. In 1432 he was appointed with two other commissioners to treat for peace with the Dauphin of France. Seven years later he was a member of another embassy sent to treat with France and he held the office of King's Secretary. In 1442 he was one of three commissioners sent to choose one of the daughters of the count of Armagnac as a wife for King Henry VI and in the next year became Keeper of the Privy Seal. In 1443 also he became bishop of Bath and Wells, which see he held until his death early in 1465. In the period 1428–43 he also sat upon several commissions to hear and determine appeals in Admiralty cases. The same variety of activities could be illustrated from the careers of countless other ecclesiastics, men such as the great Lyndwood, or Reginald Kentwood, Dean of St Paul's.

The explanation is that all these various courts and these diplomatic negotiations required a knowledge of the Roman civil law. This law was the accepted basis for the conduct of international relations and therefore for maritime cases which might involve international law. As we saw in the last lecture, its history was closely connected with that of the canon law and a knowledge of the civil law was a necessary part of the training of a canonist. The military and chivalric courts of the constable and the marshal were based upon the civil law, and Professor Plucknett has shown how, as late as the mid-

---

[1] See H. C. Maxwell-Lyte and M. C. B. Dawes, *The Register of Thomas Bekynton, Bishop of Bath and Wells 1443–1465*, Somerset Record Society, xlix and l (1934 and 1935), and a so far unpublished thesis on Beckington by Dr A. F. Judd.

fifteenth century, the common lawyers found great difficulty in dealing with what were essentially constitutional issues,[1] so that it was necessary to turn to the canonists and the civilians, with whom constitutional theories were a commonplace.

The ecclesiastical courts in the fifteenth century, it must be remembered, dealt with almost all marriage cases, probate, defamation, and sexual offences, as well as with the more strictly ecclesiastical matters. They had therefore a considerable routine business, which together with ecclesiastical administration provided an occupation for a large number of clerical lawyers. Most of the principal officers of the courts which sat in London seem nevertheless to have been employed also in government work, such as I have illustrated from the careers of Usk and Beckington.

In 1545 a statute of King Henry VIII[2] removed the limitation that jurisdiction in the ecclesiastical courts could be exercised only by clerics and opened them to married laymen being doctors created or incorporated in any University and deputed by the king or archbishop, bishop, or any other who had authority to create a chancellor, vicar-general, etc. Earlier the royal visitors of the Universities had caused the discontinuance of the canon law lectures, and consequently of the degrees, but had given encouragement to the study of the civil law. There is evidence that at the beginning of the sixteenth century a number of those who practised in the courts which required knowledge of the civil law lived in the City of London in the neighbourhood of St Paul's Cathedral, and in 1511 the then Dean of the Arches, Dr Richard Blodwell, is said to have formed them into an association. Certainly the doctors of the civil law were living

---

[1] T. F. T. Plucknett, "The Lancastrian Constitution," in *Tudor Studies presented . . . to A. F. Pollard*, edited by R. W. Seton-Watson, London (1924).

[2] 37 Henry VIII, c. 17.

together in some sort of collegiate style in the early years of the reign of Henry VIII, and by 1535 their place of residence had acquired the name of Doctors' Commons. In 1568 Dr Henry Harvey, Dean of the Arches and Master of Trinity Hall, Cambridge, acquired the lease of Mountjoy Place or House in Knightrider Street to the south of St Paul's Cathedral, to be rebuilt for the use of the Advocates and Doctors of the Arches. There a real collegiate existence was established, although the society was not legally incorporated until 1767.[1]

For some time after the rise of Doctors' Commons the courts remained in their old places, the Arches in Bow Church and the Admiralty court at Southwark, but after the Great Fire of London both courts moved to the hall of Doctors' Commons, and at some stage the Consistory court of the diocese of London also sat there. It may be added that the Marshal's court in the College of Arms was close by.

The College was governed by the Dean of the Arches as president and the advocates as fellows. They were all doctors of law of either Oxford or Cambridge who had been admitted advocate by the archbishop of Canterbury and their number was restricted. They successfully excluded clergymen, even though doctors of law, and it was also established that a Lambeth doctorate was not sufficient qualification. There were also in Doctors' Commons the proctors, who corresponded to the solicitors in other courts and prepared the cases for the advocates. A print of 1808 shows one of the courts in session. The hall was a rectangular building divided across by a screen and having an apse at one end. The court proper occupied the space between the apse and the screen, and the public could watch from beyond the

[1] For the history of Doctors' Commons see W. Senior, *Doctors' Commons and the old court of Admiralty*, London (1922), W. H. Godfrey, *London Topographical Record illustrated*, **xv**, London (1931), and *Sketches of the lives of English Civilians*, London (1804).

screen. Round the walls of the apse and on each side as far as the screen was a raised platform on which were the seats and desks of the doctors, the president occupying a slightly more exalted seat in the centre of the apse. On admission to the college each doctor was assigned a place in court which remained permanently his. On the floor of the court the proctors sat round a large table, and there also were the two registrars. In the Court of Arches the judge and advocates wore wigs, scarlet robes, hoods, and the round black doctor's cap. In the other courts they wore black gowns. The proctors wore black gowns and hoods. The numbers in the College were never very large. In 1746 there were thirty-four proctors, in 1843 twenty-six advocates.

This small group of men virtually controlled the administration of the ecclesiastical law in England. There were of course the diocesan courts, and the judges of some of these were not members of Doctors' Commons, indeed were sometimes clergymen. On the other hand some of the advocates were also chancellors of various dioceses, and from all the lower courts of the province of Canterbury an appeal lay to the Court of Arches or to one of the other provincial courts which were staffed by members of Doctors' Commons. Not even the province of York was wholly exempt, for until 1832 the final court of appeal in ecclesiastical cases was the Court of Delegates, which always included a number of civil lawyers drawn, so far as one can see, from among the advocates of Doctors' Commons. The doctors were very particular about the distinctive character of their profession and watchful for any attempts to adulterate it with untrained or common law practitioners. I have already mentioned the rejection of Lambeth degrees. In 1820 in a probate case Dr Lushington applied for a further examination of two witnesses who had already been examined in the cause, and he founded this application on an affidavit of the solicitor who had, one presumes, prepared the business in the first instance, that certain material facts had come to his knowledge since the examination of the witnesses had been completed. Dr Lushington also cited a Chancery case, Cowslade v. Cornish, as an authority to induce the Court to accede to this motion. Sir John Nicholl, sitting as Judge of the Prerogative Court of Canterbury, refused to allow application and said:

> Here the application is founded on the affidavit of the solicitor:—the solicitor is not known to the Court; the proctor who is *dominus litis*, and the party, are alone known to the Court;—and there is another reason why the proctor ought to have made the affidavit in preference to the solicitor, *viz.* that the proctor has a knowledge of the practice of the Court, and knows what circumstances ought to have weight, whereas the solicitor is a mere stranger of whom the Court knows nothing.
>
> The practice of the Court of Chancery is not analogous to our proceedings.[1]

Lest, however, one should take away the impression of a legal backwater, and that is certainly the impression given by Dickens' picture of Doctors' Commons, I propose to say something about half a dozen of the men who grew up and practised in this tradition between the Restoration of Charles II and the beginning of this century. I must preface them however by the mention of one doctor of the civil law whose achievement must surely be the most remarkable in the history of our Church, M. Nicholas Wootton, who held together uninterruptedly the deaneries of Canterbury and York for twenty-five years from the reign of King Henry VIII to that of Queen Elizabeth I.

One of those whom politics and religion had driven away from his University and who returned to Oxford in 1660 was a thirty-seven-year-old Welshman, Leoline Jenkins,[2]

---

[1] III *Phillimore*, p. 423 f.
[2] William Wynne, *The Life of Sir Leoline Jenkins*, 2 vols., London (1724).

who in 1661 proceeded to the degree of doctor of civil law and was elected Principal of Jesus College. Almost immediately he was made commissary of the deanery of the peculiar of Bridgnorth, registrar of the consistory court of Westminster Abbey, deputy professor of civil law in the University and assessor of the chancellor's court. Shortly afterwards Archbishop Sheldon made him commissary and official of the diocese of Canterbury. In 1664 Jenkins entered the College of Advocates and was quickly appointed deputy to the Dean of the Arches. In 1665 he became assistant to the judge of the admiralty court and eventually succeeded him. In 1669 he became judge of the Prerogative Court of Canterbury. From that year onwards he also became involved in a series of diplomatic activities on behalf of the government. The first, which earned him a knighthood, was to establish in France the right of Charles II to succeed to the whole personal property of Queen Henrietta Maria, in face of a counter claim by the Duchess of Orleans. The one which occupied him most and earned most fame was a long series of diplomatic negotiations with the Dutch and French, beginning with the Congress of Cologne in 1673 and ending in 1679. He was now a Privy Councillor and Member of Parliament, and from 1680 secretary of state. He resigned this office in 1684 and went into retirement, dying in the following year.

In the field of international law Jenkins was one of the most outstanding men of his time. His biographer, William Wynne, writes of him thus:

> His learned Decisions rendred his Name famous in most Parts of *Europe*, (there being at this Time almost a general War, and some of all Nations frequently Suitors to this Court) and his Answers or Reports of all Matters referr'd to him, whether from the Lords Commissioners of Prizes, Privy Council, or other great Officers of the Kingdom, were so solid and judicious, as to give universal Satisfaction, and often gain'd the Ap-

plause of those who dissented from him; because they show'd not only the Soundness of his Judgment in the particular Matters of his Profession, but a great Compass of Knowledge in the general Affairs of *Europe*, and in the ancient, as well modern Practice of other Nations. Upon any Questions or Disputes arising beyond Sea between his Majesty's Subjects and those of other Princes, they often had Recourse to Dr *Jenkins*. Even those who presided in the Seats of foreign Judicatures, in some Cases applied to him, to know how the like Point had been ruled in the Admiralty here, and his Sentences were often exemplified and obtained as Presidents there, and he had so much Humanity accompanying his Knowledge, that he never failed doing any one that sought him all the good Offices in his Power.[1]

As an ecclesiastical judge Jenkins made some useful reforms in the procedure of the courts, preventing delays and vexatious practices, and he was a steadfast upholder of the solemnity and religious tone of the courts. He was intimately concerned in the framing of one reform which unhappily was not carried into effect, namely the conversion of the High Court of Delegates into a permanent body. The practice had been, and so continued down to 1832, that a commission of delegates was appointed on the occasion of each appeal and there was therefore a lack of continuity. This in the nineteenth century was made a ground of complaint against the court and was one of the factors which led to its supersession by the Privy Council. Jenkins' reform if carried out in the seventeenth century might have avoided the unhappy history of our appeal court in the nineteenth.

The next lawyer to whom I wish to draw your attention is Sir George Lee,[2] son of a Buckinghamshire baronet, who became a Doctor of Civil Law at Oxford and an advocate in Doctors' Commons in 1729. From 1751 to 1758 he was Dean

[1] Op. cit. i, p. xiii.
[2] I *Lee*, pp. xi–xvii, and the article on Lee in the *D.N.B.*

of the Arches and Judge of the Prerogative Court of Canterbury. He was also a member of Parliament from 1733 until his death, acting with the adherents of the Prince of Wales, and becoming treasurer of the Princess's household after Prince Frederick's death. We have no evidence of diplomatic missions in which he was involved, such as we have had for the earlier lawyers, but in 1753 he was one of four signatories to an exposition of the nature and extent of the jurisdiction exercised by courts of law over ships and cargoes of neutral powers established within the territories of belligerent states. This document was an answer to a memorial from the King of Prussia and is believed to have been the joint work of Lee and the Solicitor-General, Mr Murray, later Lord Mansfield. It was described in 1833 as "the most celebrated State Paper of modern times" and referred to by Montesquieu as "une réponse sans réplique".[1]

Sir George Lee is of particular interest as two volumes of his cases begin the series of printed reports of cases in the Ecclesiastical Courts. A manuscript in the Bodleian Library [2] contains a valuable collection of opinions written by him in the thirties and forties and notes of some of the cases in which he was engaged. There were at one time in the library of his family seat at Hartwell near Aylesbury several more MS volumes of his notes of cases; that library has been dispersed in recent years and its contents are not easy to trace.[3]

From Sir George Lee we move to a far greater man, Sir William Scott, later Lord Stowell,[4] who was born in county Durham in 1745 and died at a great age in 1836, having been

[1] I *Lee*, p. xvi.

[2] MS. Eng. Misc. c. 31.

[3] The bulk of the Lee papers were sold at Sotheby's in 1939. Some of them are in the Buckinghamshire County Record Office at Aylesbury. I should welcome information about the present ownership of the rest.

[4] E. S. Roscoe, *Lord Stowell, His Life and the Development of English Prize Law*, London (1916).

Advocate of the Admiralty, Registrar of the Court of Faculties, Judge of the Consistory Court of the Diocese of London, King's Advocate, Vicar-General of the Province of Canterbury, Master of the Faculties, Judge of the High Court of the Admiralty, Member of Parliament until his elevation to the Peerage in 1821. Readers of Boswell will remember him as a member of Dr Johnson's circle. Lord Stowell's reputation was made first and foremost in the Admiralty Court, for during the greater part of the period of his judgeship, 1798–1827, England was at war, and innumerable cases of great difficulty came before him. In 1799 he stated the principles on which he approached his task.

> I trust, he said, that it has not escaped my anxious recollection for one moment, what it is that the duty of my station calls for from me—namely, to consider myself as stationed here, not to deliver occasional and shifting opinions to serve present purposes of particular national interest, but to administer with indifference that justice which the Law of Nations holds out, without distinction, to independent states, some happening to be neutral and some to be belligerent.[1]

He carried this to very great lengths as appears from other passages in his judgements in which he seems prepared to set the Law of Nations above Acts of Parliament.

> This, he said in 1807, is a Court of the Law of Nations, though sitting here under the authority of the King of Great Britain. It belongs to other nations as well as to our own; and what foreigners have a right to demand from it is the administration of the law of nations, simply, and exclusively of principles borrowed from our own municipal jurisprudence, to which, it is well known, they have at all times expressed no inconsiderable repugnance.[2]

[1] E. S. Roscoe, op. cit. p. 41.
[2] T. E. Holland, *Studies in International Law*, Oxford (1898), p. 196.

Four years later he states that "these two propositions, that the Court is bound to administer the Law of Nations, and that it is bound to enforce the King's Orders in Council, are not at all inconsistent with each other", because these orders and instructions will always conform themselves, under the given circumstances, to the principles of the unwritten law which is binding on the Court. He declines to speculate as to the course to be followed in the case of a conflict because he could not "without extreme indecency, presume that any such emergency would happen".[1] Nine volumes contain the Admiralty decisions of Lord Stowell and they are the basis of the modern English prize law. Professor Holland described him as "the most eminent judge who ever presided in a prize court".

The Ecclesiastical Courts, having already a more developed system, offered less scope for Lord Stowell's abilities, but even there he left his mark. The reader of the recent Report on the Church and the Nullity of Marriage may perhaps have noted that he is there cited for an important principle in connection with the law of Nullity.[2] The spirit in which he approached this part of his work is perhaps best indicated by these words from the conclusion of a contested faculty case:

> One great object of the Court in Parish contests, is to quiet them as soon as may be, and the Court indulges the hope, that moderation on its part in not condemning the objecting parties in costs, may teach them moderation in their future intercourse with their neighbours and fellow-parishioners; and on these grounds, I think I shall best consult the interests of the Parish, by decreeing the Faculty, but not condemning the opposers in costs.[3]

The search for moderation and equity inspires all his judgements, as does his great learning, even though on occasion

---

[1] T. E. Holland, op. cit. p. 197.
[2] *The Church and the Law of Nullity of Marriage*, London (1955), pp. 27 f.   [3] I *Haggard*, p. 197.

the latter may seem to be unduly paraded. In a case arising out of the desire of a Mr Gilbert to bury his wife in an iron coffin in the churchyard of St Andrew's Holborn one feels that it was hardly necessary for the judge to say: "Before entering into the immediate question, it may not be entirely useless or foreign to remark, that the most ancient modes of disposing of the bodies of the dead mentioned by history, are by burial or by burning, of which the former appears to be the more ancient," and then to continue for half a dozen pages of history of burial practices before arriving at the substance of which the coffin may be made and the fee to be charged for one whose decay will be slow.[1]

Before leaving Lord Stowell I cannot forbear to quote some sentences from his judgement in a case brought by the Curate of St Botolph, Aldersgate, against the churchwardens who had obstructed and prohibited "the singing or chanting by the parish clerk and children of the ward, and congregation, accompanied by the organ".[2] What, apparently, the churchwardens had objected to was the singing at morning and afternoon service of the *Gloria Patri* in prose at the end of the psalms and in other parts of the service, and possibly also to the singing of part of the psalms. For them it was argued that though singing part of the psalms is properly practised in cathedrals it is not so in parish churches. "No law," says Lord Stowell, "has been adduced to this effect, but modern usage alone has been relied on; and it is said that such has been the practice from the time of the Reformation. This, however, is not supported by any particular statement of fact or authority." He therefore indulged in a short historical disquisition on the use of music in Church, observing by the way that

The *Calvinistic* Churches, of which it has sometimes been harshly said, "that they think to find religion wherever they do

[1] II *Haggard*, pp. 340 ff.   [2] I *Haggard*, pp. 170–80.

not find the Church of Rome," have discarded it entirely, with a strong attachment to plain congregational melody,—and that perhaps not always of the most harmonious kind.

From his history he concludes that

under the statutes of the Reformation, and the usage explanatory of them, it is recommended, that the ancient hymns (by which he means the prose psalms) should be used in the Liturgy, or rather that they should be preferred to any others: though certainly to perform them by a select band with complex music, very inartificially applied, as in many of the Churches of the country, is a practice not more reconcileable to good taste than to edification.

The conclusion of his judgement is notable:

If it be urged that there is any incongruity in this, I answer, that I have to discuss a question of illegality, not of incongruity. It is true, indeed, that what is obsolete is liable to the objection of novelty, and likewise, that it has been tried and laid aside. The Court would not therefore advise the Minister to introduce what may be liable to such remarks, against the inclination of the Parishioners, and the approbation of the Bishop. But this is a matter of expediency and discretion, which the Court must leave to the consideration of others. Having thus declared that the Churchwardens are not entitled to interfere, and that the practice is legal, it may be expected I should admit these articles. I am certainly authorized to do so; but I shall suspend their admission till the first day of next term, recommending an accommodation to the parties, and only intimating that the general sense of the Parish, properly obtained, will weigh very much with the Court in the further consideration of this subject.

When the case next came on the curate declared that he wished to proceed no further and so, one hopes, the judge's wisdom restored peace to the parish.

We turn from Lord Stowell to a name celebrated in three generations of English legal history, that of Phillimore. The first of the name to be prominent in this branch of learning was Joseph Phillimore (1775–1855),[1] who became a doctor of civil law of Oxford and was admitted Advocate in 1804. In 1809 he became regius professor of civil law at Oxford, chancellor of the diocese of Oxford, and judge of the admiralty court of the Cinque Ports. Many years later he was appointed King's Advocate in the admiralty court, and chancellor of the dioceses of Worcester, and Bristol, judge of the consistory court of Gloucester, and commissary of the dean and chapter of St Paul's. He edited the reports of Sir George Lee's cases and three volumes of cases in the ecclesiastical courts at Doctors' Commons 1809–21. In 1840 he was elected a Fellow of the Royal Society. Joseph Phillimore was clearly a man of less distinction than Lord Stowell and Sir George Lee, but he exemplifies well the close connection which was maintained between Doctors' Commons and the Universities. Phillimore remained regius professor at Oxford until his death, he played a distinguished part in University life, and in 1834 he received an honorary LL.D. from Cambridge.

Three of Joseph Phillimore's sons are to be found in the *Dictionary of National Biography*. The eldest, John George, was called to the bar at Lincoln's Inn and later became reader in civil law and jurisprudence at the Middle Temple, and reader in constitutional law and legal history to the Inns of Court. Two writings of his have survived which give an historical account of the canon law and its influence, but his practice clearly lay in a different field from that of his father. The fifth son, Greville, became a clergyman, was one of the editors of the "parish Hymn Book", and published sermons and novels. The third son, Robert Joseph,[2] is the one who most deserves our attention.

He followed his father's profession, becoming doctor of

[1] See *D.N.B.*
[2] In addition to the *D.N.B.* see T. E. Holland, op. cit. pp. 300–1.

civil law in 1838, Advocate in Doctors' Commons in 1839, commissary to the deans and chapters of Westminster and St Paul's, official to the archdeaconries of London and Middlesex, chancellor of the dioceses of Chichester, Salisbury, and Oxford, and eventually judge of the high court of admiralty and Dean of the Arches. He was for five years a member of parliament, and at the end of his life judge of the probate division of the high court. He wrote a large work, *Commentaries on International Law*, which became a standard authority, and his importance in the development of English Prize Law was considerable. In this sphere it is interesting to find him asserting the same doctrine as Lord Stowell as to the duty of a Prize Court to obey the principles of International Law rather than Orders in Council which might seem inconsistent with them.

> It is clear, he said, that it has never been the doctrine of the British Prize Courts that, because they sit under the authority of the Crown, the Crown has authority to prescribe to them rules which violate International Law.[1]

In his Commentaries he writes:

> If he (i.e. Lord Stowell) had not so considered them (i.e. considered the Orders in Council to be inconsistent with International Law), and nevertheless had executed them, he would have incurred the same guilt, and deserved the same reprehension, as the judge of a municipal Court, who executed by his sentence an edict of the legislature which plainly violated the law written by the Creator upon the conscience of his creature.[1]

As regards Prize Courts something of this position was confirmed by the Privy Council in the case of *The Zamora* in 1916,[2] but one doubts whether the further reference to the judges of the Common Law courts would find much re-

[1] Holland, op. cit. p. 198.
[2] D. L. Keir and F. H. Lawson, *Cases in Constitutional Law*, 3rd ed. (1948), pp. 66 f.

sponse to-day. When Phillimore died in 1885 Professor T. E. Holland wrote in the *Revue de Droit International*: "La science du droit international vient de perdre un des plus vénérés d'entre les jurisconsultes qui l'ont cultivée." [1]

Phillimore was also the editor, or rather remodeller, of one of the most widely used text-books of Ecclesiastical Law, that originally written by Dr Richard Burn in 1760, and both as an advocate and as a judge he was involved in a number of the most important and controversial cases of the second half of the last century. In the early 1840s there was a proposal to throw open the practice in the Courts at Doctors' Commons to the generality of barristers, and Robert Phillimore in 1843 published a pamphlet in defence of his profession against this attack.[2] At the same time he was by no means blind to the need for reform in the administration of the ecclesiastical law. In his pamphlet he signalized two evils, the multitude of small courts of Peculiar jurisdiction (it was calculated that in 1832 there were 386 ecclesiastical courts in England), and the fact that in a number of dioceses the judges were persons without proper legal training.

> Whatever be the fate of the bill now pending in Parliament, (he wrote) I trust that these defects will be cured, that the Peculiars will be abolished, and that the ancient and proper qualifications will be required for the Chancellors. I am fully convinced that an officer so qualified would be of the greatest service to the Bishops, preventing many unseemly collisions with his clergy, while in no way derogating from his authority; satisfying the jealousy of the common law in all matters of interference with freehold tenure, restoring much of the whole-some and ancient discipline of our Church, and rendering impossible any approach to such conflicts as now rend in pieces the Presbytery of Scotland.[3]

[1] Holland, op. cit. p. 300.
[2] R. J. Phillimore, *The study of the civil and canon law in its relation to the state, the church, and the universities*, London, 1843.
[3] Op. cit. p. 51.

49

During his five years in Parliament he was the sole or part author of three important measures of reform in the ecclesiastical law. In 1854 he secured the amendment of the law relating to simony and the sale of next presentations, and in 1856 he was responsible for the act which abolished the jurisdiction of the ecclesiastical courts in suits for defamation. The small but far-reaching measure on which he particularly prided himself, however, was an act of 1854 which enabled the ecclesiastical courts to take evidence *viva voce* instead of by the cumbrous and not very satisfactory method of written depositions being taken from the witnesses by an examiner without the presence of counsel.[1]

Robert Phillimore is the last of this group of lawyers who grew up in Doctors' Commons, but in order to round off the story of the family I must mention briefly his son, Walter George Frank, who became the first Lord Phillimore.[2] Although Doctors' Commons had ceased to exist before he was twenty he nevertheless specialized in ecclesiastical and international law. His appointment in 1897 to be a judge of the Queen's Bench division was unexpected and not altogether successful, but when he became a lord justice of appeal and a Privy Councillor in 1913 his abilities and his knowledge found full scope. Lord Sankey wrote of him in this sphere that "his work justified his claim to be considered as one of the great lawyers of his generation". In 1917 and 1918 he was chairman of a committee which considered early schemes for the League of Nations, and in 1920 was a member of the committee which drew up the statute constituting the Permanent Court of International Justice at The Hague. He was an active member of the Church Assembly in the mid-twenties and one of the chief authors of the scheme for clergy

[1] *The Principal Ecclesiastical Judgments delivered in the Court Arches 1867 to 1875 by the Right Hon. Sir Robert Phillimore, D.C.L.*, London (1876), p. viii.
[2] *D.N.B.*, Supplement 1901–30.

pensions. His appointment as a judge of the high court cut short his career in the ecclesiastical courts as in the admiralty court, but he had already made his mark in both those spheres. As Chancellor of the diocese of Lincoln he defended Bishop King before the court of the Archbishop of Canterbury, and he was responsible for the second edition of his father's new version of Burn's *Ecclesiastical Law*, a book which generally goes under his name and is still of great value. He died in 1929.

In his *Concise History of the Common Law* Professor Plucknett writes:

> The nineteenth century is occupied almost continuously with changes in the judicial system, many of them individually of slight extent, and in the earlier half uncertain of their ultimate aim. In the middle of the century the experience obtained was sufficiently definite to make it clear that a policy of detailed readjustment was inadequate, and so the more thorough policy of the judicature acts eventually triumphed.[1]

Between the various courts of common law and equity there was much unnecessary separation and conflict of jurisdiction over the same subject matter. Even Blackstone had written in 1768:

> Sure there cannot be a greater solecism, than that in two sovereign independent courts, established in the same country, exercising concurrent jurisdiction, and over the same subject matter, there should exist in a single instance two different rules of property clashing with or contradicting each other.[2]

And Bentham said:

> A man who owes a sum of money which it is not agreeable to him to pay, fights a battle so long as he can on the ground

[1] T. F. T. Plucknett, *A Concise History of the Common Law*, 4th ed., London (Butterworth & Co. Ltd., 1948), p. 197.

[2] Quoted by W. S. Holdsworth, *A History of English Law*, i, 5th ed., London (1931), p. 635. See this work for this and the following paragraphs.

of common law, and when he has no more ground to stand upon he applies to a court of equity to stop the proceedings in the common law court, and the equity court stops them of course.[1]

We have already seen that the multitude of courts of Peculiars laid the system of the ecclesiastical courts open to attack, and the reformers were not slow to pick on other real or imagined flaws in it. In 1823 and 1924 there were reports on the courts of the Archbishop of Canterbury and the Bishop of London, and in 1832 on the ecclesiastical courts in general. These were followed by a number of reforms of which the abolition of the Peculiars and the transfer of the Final Appellate jurisdiction from the Delegates to the Privy Council were the chief.

In the middle of the century the attack on the church courts became involved with attacks on the theological domination of society, and in 1853 a commission recommended radical changes in the method of dealing with matrimonial cases. At about the same time it was urged that the probate jurisdiction be taken away from the church. Accordingly an Act of 1857 set up a court of Probate, presided over by a judge who was to be the same person as the judge of the court of admiralty and to exercise the jurisdiction which had formerly been exercised by the ecclesiastical courts. In the same year the matrimonial jurisdiction was taken away also and vested in a new court whose judges were the Lord Chancellor, the chief justices, the judge of the Probate court, and certain of the common law judges. For some cases the Probate judge could sit alone. An appeal to the House of Lords from the Probate court was provided in 1857 and from the Matrimonial court in 1868.

The position of the new Probate judge to some extent held together and provided continuity with the jurisdictions formerly managed by the civilians, but in 1857 it was clearly

[1] Quoted by Holdsworth, op. cit. p. 635.

envisaged that they as a body would cease to exist, for the College was empowered to surrender its Charter and to sell all its real and personal property and divide the proceeds among the Fellows.[1] When they began to consider this it seems that only one or two made any protest. Dr John Lee [2] tried to persuade his colleagues that they were merely trustees for life to their college and that Doctors' Commons ought to be preserved, and developed into a foundation available for graduates in law from any university in the United Kingdom who desired to study the Roman civil law. When they refused to support him he appealed to the five Visitors of the College and to the government. One of the five Visitors was the Lord Chancellor, and in 1859 with a change of government this office was held by Lord Campbell, who in evidence before the ecclesiastical courts commission of 1832 had said:

> I have the most sincere respect for the civilians as a body, and I should think that any alteration of the law that would not preserve the learning which is now to be found among the civilians would be very objectionable.[3]

Whether it was too late, whether the opposition was too determined, or whether national and international crises absorbed the attention of legislators to the exclusion of all else, we cannot say. In 1861 the Advocates sold by auction their magnificent library to whose support every bishop on his appointment had been accustomed to contribute £20, their manuscripts and their portraits, and in 1862 the College estate. Five years later the buildings had disappeared.

The practice in such business as remained to the ecclesiastical courts was gradually thrown open to the whole legal profession, but in 1872 Sir Robert Phillimore, now Dean of

[1] For the attempts to save Doctors' Commons and its destruction see the *London Topographical Record*, xv.

[2] Appropriately he was of the same family as Sir George Lee, and an owner of Hartwell House.

[3] Quoted in R. J. Phillimore, op. cit. pp. 38 f.

the Arches, observed in an open letter to the Archbishop of Canterbury that the number of experts for ecclesiastical cases was so small that some of them commanded very high fees and that this was chiefly responsible for the considerable expense of suits of this kind.[1] In 1883 another Royal Commission reported on the subject of the Ecclesiastical courts, and I take the following extracts from the examination of witnesses before it.

The Archbishop of Canterbury: It is not very easy to find ecclesiastical judges now-a-days, is it?

The Rt. Hon. A. J. B. Beresford-Hope, M.P.: Not at all so. That comes so much from the dearth of ecclesiastical lawyers.[2]

The Abp. of Canterbury: The difficulty, of course, is in finding a sufficient number of persons who have given their attention to the study of ecclesiastical law?

The Rev. Malcolm MacColl: No doubt.

The Abp.: And the alterations in the courts which have made ecclesiastical law no longer what it once was, a lucrative profession with a career of its own?

Mr MacColl: Quite so. At present I suppose that the race of ecclesiastical lawyers is pretty well extinct, and there is no possibility of its being revived.

The Abp.: It has not quite come to that, I hope, as yet, looking round the table, but still they are in process of extinction?

Mr MacColl: Yes I mean that.[3]

The Abp. of Canterbury: Am I right in thinking that since Doctors' Commons has been abolished there are no civilians as a separate class?

Canon Liddon: I believe that that is the case. And I hope it is not impertinent to say it is a great misfortune. The Church has her rules of discipline and procedure just as much as the

[1] R. J. Phillimore, *Clergy Discipline, a letter to the Archbishop of Canterbury*, London (1872).

[2] *Report of the Commissioners appointed to inquire into the Constitution and Working of the Ecclesiastical Courts*, London (1883), ii, p. 308.

[3] Ibid. ii, p. 311.

State. What we call the ecclesiastical law is the historical accumulation of the rules and laws which have regulated in other centuries the Church's life, and we cannot hope to sweep that away and to substitute for it mere civil law without getting into serious complications . . . as your Grace is so good as to ask for my opinion, I must say that the ruin with which ecclesiastical law as a subject and ecclesiastical lawyers as a profession are threatened, does seem to be full of danger to some of the best interests of the Church.[1]

L. T. Dibdin, Esq.: At present, since Doctors' Commons has been abolished, there is really no method of teaching or preserving a knowledge of the ecclesiastical law in the country at all.[2]

To these I may add the comment of a modern writer on the failure of Dr Lee's efforts to save Doctors' Commons:

Within half a century his foresight and public spirit were amply vindicated. As the interdependence of the British realms, with their varied systems of jurisprudence, became clearer, as international relations grew more complicated and international law more important, the wisdom of his contention of the need for such a college was revealed. The sale of Doctors' Commons involved much more than the destruction of a venerable building; it ruined an institution which might have rendered great services to the British Empire and to the world.[3]

Doctors' Commons has gone beyond recall, but it is right that we should remember the services of these men to the Church of which they were members. It was a great thing that

[1] *Report of the Commissioners appointed to inquire into the Constitution and Working of the Ecclesiastical Courts*, London (1883), ii, p. 361 f.

[2] Ibid. ii, p. 371.

[3] *London Topographical Record*, xv, p. 86 (London Topographical Society). It is difficult to reconcile Dickens' picture of Doctors' Commons with the impressions gained from a study of the reports of cases in the Ecclesiastical Courts.

our ecclesiastical law should have been administered for so long by men whose occupation was also with a law based upon principles of morality and consent rather than upon the commands of a sovereign. More than most systems the law of the Church must rest upon moral authority rather than coercion and those who administer it must have large minds.

III

In this third lecture I wish first to return to the subject with which we ended the first, namely the nature and content of the law of the Church. The Act of Parliament which embodied the submission of the clergy and provided for the restraint of appeals to Rome, in 1534, envisaged the setting up of a commission of thirty-two persons to revise "such canons, constitutions, and ordinances, as heretofore have been made by the clergy of this realm". It is by no means certain that this revision was intended to cover the whole body of the medieval canon law, although fairly clearly it was to cover everything contained in Lyndwood. The Act further contained the following proviso:

> Provided also, that such canons, constitutions, ordinances, and synodals provincial being already made, which be not contrariant or repugnant to the laws, statutes, and customs of this realm, nor to the damage or hurt of the king's prerogative royal, shall more still be used and executed as they were afore the making of this Act, till such time as they be viewed, searched, or otherwise ordered and determined by the said two-and-thirty persons, or the more part of them, according to the tenor, form, and effect of this present Act.[1]

As is well known, the commission's work, although published as the *Reformatio Legum Ecclesiasticarum*, never received the authority of either Church or State, so that the proviso has continued as the operative part of the statute to the present day.

At the beginning of the last century in a case concerning the refusal of an incumbent to bury the infant child of two of

[1] 25 Henry VIII, cap. 19.

his parishioners who were Dissenters, the Dean of the Arches, Sir John Nicholl, gave the following definition of the law of the Church of England:

The Law of the Church of England, and its history, are to be deduced from the ancient general Canon Law—from the particular constitutions made in this country to regulate the English Church—from our own Canons—from the Rubric, and from any acts of Parliament that may have passed upon the subject; and the whole may be illustrated, also, by the writings of eminent persons.[1]

Sir John proceeded to apply this definition to the subject of the validity of lay baptism. If the ancient Canon Law were inquired into, he maintained, it would appear that, from the earliest times, the use of water with the invocation of the name of the Father, of the Son, and of the Holy Ghost, was held to be the essence of baptism; that baptism, so administered, even by a layman or a woman, was valid; and that a person so baptized was not to be baptized again. After mentioning in passing the Scriptural foundation of the law of the Church in this respect, he said: "Now, conformable to what has been already stated will be found the text of the canon law," and he proceeded to quote eight canons from the fourth distinction of the third part of Gratian's *Decretum*, concluding: "It is perfectly clear that, according to the general Canon Law, though regular baptism was by a Bishop or Priest, yet if administered by a Laic, or by a Heretic or Schismatic, it was valid baptism."

From the general canon law the learned judge passed to the legatine and provincial constitutions of England. The constitutions, he said, "have been collected by the very eminent English Canonist, Lyndwood; who has written a very learned commentary or gloss upon them, which is also of high authority in all courts administering the ecclesiastical law of this country". He had no difficulty in showing

[1] III *Phillimore*, p. 276.

that both the legatine and the provincial constitutions re-
inforced what he had deduced to be the general canon law on
this point.

The question as to whether any change in this had been
made by the Church of England at the time of the Reformation required more detailed examination, and the next ten
pages of the judgement are occupied by an inquiry into the
rubrics of the baptismal rites and the discussions concerning
them from the reign of Edward VI to the Restoration. Here
the judge found himself constrained to examine the questions
which the Prayer Book directs the minister to put to those
who bring a child to church after it has been baptized
privately at home, the questions which are introduced by the
words "Because some things essential to this Sacrament may
happen to be omitted through fear or haste in such times of
extremity", and concern the matter and the words employed
in the rite.

> If any doubt could be made upon what is meant by the Rubric
> in this respect (he says), it would be cleared up most satis-
> factorily by adverting to the old law upon the subject; and by
> the old law (as has been already stated) it was the use of the
> water and the invocation of the Holy Trinity that was essential
> to the baptism; those, as Lyndwood has explained, were the
> *duo necessaria.*
> Again,—if every thing has been "done as it ought to be".
> What is meant by the phrase "done as it ought to be" is ex-
> plained, by adverting to the commentary of Lyndwood; for he
> has stated in his gloss the terms *rite ministratus*, *legitime factum*,
> and *forma debita* to mean the use of water and the form of
> words: this can therefore leave no doubt what was the meaning
> of the Rubric, thus illustrated as it is by reference to the ancient
> law and to Lyndwood.[1]

Finally he considers the practice of the Church of England
since the Restoration and points out that many who were

[1] III *Phillimore*, pp. 289 f.

confirmed and ordained in the years following that event must have been baptized by persons who were not episcopally ordained and that there was no direction for their re-baptism before the confirmation or ordination.

The practice also, as I understand (he says), has always been, if Presbyterians or any other Dissenters from the Church of England have come over to that Church, and have become members of it, nay, have become ministers of it, they have never been rebaptized. Their baptism being with water and with the invocation of the Trinity, has always been considered as a sufficient initiation into the Christian Church to qualify them to join that Church, to become members, and even to become ministers, of the Church of England.[1]

This case forms a good illustration of the way in which the pre-Reformation canon law was used to supply the background and explanation of particular directions of the Prayer Book. There are, however, spheres of the law which are governed chiefly by pre-Reformation enactments. Thus, in 1848, a clerk was charged with having accepted a benefice with cure of souls whilst in possession of another benefice with cure of souls without dispensation, and it was alleged that by Canon 29 of the fourth Lateran Council of 1215 he was *ipso jure* deprived of the first living. In the judgement Sir Herbert Jenner Fust said:

The first of the articles sets forth the law, namely, that by decree of the Council of Lateran, when any person in possession of a benefice with cure of souls shall accept another like benefice, the former becomes void, that is, he loses that benefice, and that is the law of this country at this time. The Statute of Henry VIII. does not affect this law, except that it makes the other living voidable; that is, by sentence, or void by presentation of the patron.[2]

[1] III *Phillimore*, pp. 293 f.
[2] Quoted in R. J. Phillimore, *The Principal Ecclesiastical Judgments delivered in the Court of Arches 1867 to 1875* (1876), pp. 36 f.

This was particularly so in the matter of procedure, as appears from a somewhat unexpected source, namely Archbishop Tennison's judgement on Bishop Watson of St David's, who appeared before him in 1699 on charges of simony and some other offences. The archbishop states that he proposes to show in general what proof the Ecclesiastical Law requires in a case of simony and he says:

As for ye Proof wch y^t *Law requires*, In this Case, It accepts even of ye Testimony of a *Harlot*, & of *Signa* wch have any probability in them. And this (saith y^t great Lawyer *Hostiensis* upon 5 of ye Decretals) is peculiar to y^t Crime of Simony; whereas, in other Crimes, Proofs are required wch are clearer y^n ye Light.[1]

The marginal note refers to folio 142 of the Lyons edition of the commentary of Hostiensis on the fifth book of the Decretals of Gregory IX. It may well be that this case deserves the reservation which Lord Stowell applied to one of some twenty years later which was cited to him, that it "took place in times of party ferment, and is of smaller authority on that account",[2] and yet it cannot be entirely passed over, for one of the archbishop's assessors was the great Edmund Gibson, who no doubt assisted with the canon law references. At any rate it can be supported by cases later in the eighteenth century upon which no such aspersions can be cast.

In a suit for the restitution of conjugal rights brought before Sir George Lee in 1753 it was objected that the petitioner, a Mrs Grant, could not sue because she was excommunicated by the constitution against clandestine marriages, contained in Lyndwood. The marriage in question had taken place at the Fleet without the proper forms and was therefore clandestine. Appeal was made to an earlier case of Colli *v.* Colli, which in various ways had lasted from 1742 to 1746,

[1] Bodley MS. Rawlinson B. 380, f. 261.
[2] I *Haggard*, p. 175.

and in which at one stage also it had been argued that Mrs Colli could not sue because she was excommunicate by reason of clandestine marriage. In that case the judge, Dr Andrew, had upheld the submission. It so happened that Sir George Lee had been counsel in the Colli case, and his notes of it are in a MS. volume of his in the Bodleian Library to which I referred in my second lecture. In them we have a skeleton of the arguments on both sides and of the judgement on this particular stage of the case. The whole discussion was conducted on the basis of the statements of pre-Reformation and post-Reformation continental canonists and civilians, and the judge quoted them as authorities in his judgement.[1] Lee was dissatisfied with the conclusion of the Colli case and took the opportunity of the one which came before him in 1753 to rule in a contrary direction,[2] but there is no reason to think that he was dissatisfied with the authorities alleged.

No one, I think, can read the published reports of the cases in the ecclesiastical courts down to the middle of the last century without being struck by the familiarity of the advocates not only with the medieval canon law and its commentators, but also with the continental canonists of the sixteenth and seventeenth centuries such as Sanchez, the great authority on the law of marriage, Pierre de Marca, the Gallican archbishop of Paris, and Van Espen, the celebrated doctor of Louvain. The Ecclesiastical Law in England was not regarded as an isolated system, but as a part, albeit with its own special rules, of a much greater system and one which might be illuminated and assisted by works of canonists in other lands. Down to the second quarter of the nineteenth century Parliamentary statutes and the canons of Convocation covered only a part, and that scarcely the largest part, of the

[1] Bodley, MS. Eng. Misc. c. 31, ff. 182–79 (the order of the pages here goes backward).
[2] I *Lee*, p. 593.

field in which the ecclesiastical lawyers moved. What seems to us a vague expression, "the general Ecclesiastical Law", was something quite definite and emphatic to them because they were familiar with the jurisprudence of centuries, the traditional usage of Western Christendom. That this was something quite distinct from the common law was recognized by the most eminent among the common lawyers themselves, and in the early days of the Judicial Committee of the Privy Council we find one of them, Sir James Parke, later Lord Wensleydale, saying: "The proceedings of the Ecclesiastical Court are not governed by the rules of the Common Law, or by any analogies which they furnish."[1]

In the first lecture I spoke of the place of custom in the medieval canon law. In connection with the present revision of the canons there has been much reference to the importance of custom, and in the session of the Church Assembly held in February, 1956, one of the most eminent of our chancellors stated emphatically that the principle of the forty years' custom was not a part of the law of England.[2] Whether he meant to suggest that no appeal to the old canonical principle could be entertained in an English ecclesiastical court is not clear, but it seems worth while to discuss the subject a little. This is, I think, the more necessary in view of what is said in the Report of the Canon Law Commission (of which the learned chancellor just mentioned was a member). On p. 64 of the Report we find these remarks about a judgement delivered in the House of Lords in 1868:

This judgment emphasizes the two important points, that post-Reformation custom continues pre-Reformation custom as law and that post-Reformation contrary custom abrogates pre-Reformation custom and deprives it of the force of law, but

[1] Moore, *Privy Council Reports*, p. 399.
[2] Church Assembly, Spring Session, 1956, Report of Proceedings, London (1956), xxxvi, p. 34.

it must not be thought that these principles do not extend to post-Reformation custom. The rule of ordinary English law that a custom to be enforceable must be shown or be presumed to have been in existence in the year 1189 (a rule frequently tempered in practice) is not a rule of Canon Law. By Canon Law, so far as length of time is concerned, the test is: "Can it be shown by clear evidence that the custom has been followed for an uninterrupted period of at least forty years?" The comparative shortness of this period makes it possible for post-Reformation customs to be treated as enforceable, and just as new customs can in this way acquire the force of law, so can old customs previously enforceable lose their validity by a contrary custom of at least forty years' duration. Contrary custom, it should be explained, is more than mere non-user; "it is necessary that the omission be a true one, that is, one in opposition to a legal obligation; it must also occur at the time for which the precept commanded the action, since the omission of an action when no action was obligatory is no indication of a will to disregard a law, or to refuse to accept it, as is self-evident."

Unhappily the only authority to which the Report refers for these remarks about the forty years' custom is the Counter-Reformation Jesuit Francisco Suarez, from whose works the last sentence is quoted.

It is abundantly clear that there are sections of the ecclesiastical law to which in our courts the rules of the common law requiring immemorial custom have been fairly consistently applied. This is of course the case with tithe actions, which were to a great extent tried in the common law courts. The old text-books are explicit on this point, and I will quote one of them as an example, Sir Simon Degge's *Parson's Counsellor* first published in 1676. In Part II, chapter 13, where he is discussing custom in relation to the law of tithes he writes:

But I must here observe to the Reader, that though the Civil and Ecclesiastical Laws do in some Cases take notice of Custom and Prescription; yet in this they differ from the Common Law, that they allow a usage for forty years to be a good proof of a Custom or Prescription, grounding their Judgments upon a decretal Epistle of Pope *Alexander* the Third, *Anno Domini* 1180. But this Kingdom never allowed of that Epistle, or yielded any obedience thereunto: So that as well in Spiritual as Temporal Prescriptions and Customs, if they come to be tried at Common Law, as all Prescriptions concerning Tythes must be, they must be proved to have been used beyond the memory of any man to the contrary; for if any man living, or any Authentick Record, or other evidence prove it was otherwise at any time since the first year of *Richard* the first, which was *Anno Domini* 1189 the Custom or Prescription fails.[1]

It seems also to have been held in the ecclesiastical courts that in default of a faculty immemorial usage is necessary to establish a right to a particular seat in church. In 1798 Lord Stowell declared that "all private rights in pews must be held under a faculty, or by prescription, which presumes a faculty," [2] and in 1811 Sir John Nicholl said in a suit for "perturbation of seat" as it was called:

A possessory right is sufficient to maintain a suit against a mere disturber;—the fact of possession implies either the actual or virtual authority of those having power to place. The disturber must shew that he has been placed there by this authority,—or must justify his disturbance by shewing a paramount right,—a right paramount to the ordinary itself; namely, a faculty by which the ordinary has parted with the right: or if there be no proof of a faculty,—there may be proof of prescription, and such immemorial usage as presumes the grant of a faculty.[3]

The same principle has also been held to apply to fees, as appears from a case before Sir George Lee in 1753. Here the

[1] S. Degge, *The Parson's Counsellor with the Law of Tythes or Tything*, London (1685 edn.), pp. 217 f.
[2] I *Haggard*, p. 317.
[3] I *Phillimore*, p. 324.

vicar of South Petherton, Somerset, claimed that an immemorial custom established the obligation of every spinster or single woman, being an inhabitant or parishioner of South Petherton, to pay to the vicar an offering of five shillings on the occasion of her marriage, whether she was married at South Petherton or not. Dr Pinfold, appearing for one of the inhabitants who had refused to pay this fee, pointed out that whereas the original statement, the libel, said that the custom was immemorial, the witnesses spoke only to a short time. Dr Paul in reply for the vicar said that a statute of Edward I had provided that suits for oblations should be in the spiritual court, that the payment of this fee was an ecclesiastical custom, *and therefore it was sufficient to prove it for forty years.* Dr Bettesworth, opposing for the parishioner, also said: "They should shew the custom was originally good, and has been for forty years a custom; it must be reasonable." Giving judgement Sir George Lee pointed out that notwithstanding the statute of Edward I, if the custom was denied, the common law courts would issue a prohibition for the case to be tried at common law, and alleged a recent case in the King's Bench in which he himself had appeared, in which a prohibition was granted to stay a suit in the Ecclesiastical Court for customary Easter offerings, and the custom was denied. The matter being therefore subject to the cognizance of the common law, Sir George thought himself bound to determine it in accordance with the principles of that law, but in the judgement he said,

clearly by the common law this custom is not proved, for it is not sufficiently proved even by the ecclesiastical law, which required a usage for forty years to be proved; but here no instance has been given of paying the fee demanded for above twenty-one years; and therefore I thought the custom was not proved, but if it had been proved, the custom would be unreasonable, for no ecclesiastical law warrants a demand of a fee where no service is done, and . . . in similar cases, the temporal

66

courts had determined, that a custom to pay a fee where no service was done, was unreasonable. . . . [1]

While these examples show clearly that certain ecclesiastical matters have been subject to the common law rules regarding custom, the last of them shows equally clearly that in the middle of the eighteenth century it was recognized in the ecclesiastical courts that the old principle of the forty years' custom would still operate, and this is borne out by an Opinion given by Sir George Lee in 1748 on a case involving the liability of an Impropriator to repair the chancel of Newark parish church. I quote the first question put to him, and his answer.

> Q. 1. If the Spiritual Court proceeds by Custom time out of mind this ordination will contradict such Custom, but if they go by a Custom of 40 years etc. continuance, will they support this Custom against the authority & express words of the Ordination of Endowment, or can this Custom be ever supposed to have a legal or reasonable commencement.
>
> Answer. In many cases a usage of 40 years will make a Prescription by the Ecclesiastical Law but I think this Custom cannot be supposed to have a legal or reasonable Commencement, & its being contrary not only to the general Law but also to the express words of the Ordination of Endowment I am of Opinion it will not be supported in the Spiritual Court, vid. Watson 394.[2]

The text-books of the English ecclesiastical law do not for the most part deal with matters of this kind; they have no section on general principles such as custom, dispensation, the reckoning of time and so forth, all of which are commonplaces to the continental canonist. There is, however, one book where a discussion of this subject is to be found, and that is in the *Parergon Juris Canonici Anglicani* [3] of John Ayliffe.

---

[1] I *Lee*, pp. 387–98.   [2] MS. Eng. Misc. c. 51, f. 211.
[3] Published in London, 1726.

This writer,[1] who was born in 1676, was an Oxford doctor of law and a Wykehamist. Down to 1710 he practised as a proctor in the chancellor's court and, he tells us, "had a prospect of succeeding to some chancellorship or other preferment in the church of like nature". However, he was a Whig in a predominantly Tory society, and came into conflict with the authorities of the University. He is said to have threatened to pistol the Warden of New College, and certainly some incident took place which caused him to resign his fellowship and be deprived of his degrees. Undoubtedly he belongs to Lord Stowell's "times of party ferment", but this does not detract from his learning, and his party connections would have disposed him to attack rather than to defend ecclesiastical pretensions. Certain it is that his book on the canon law was much quoted in the courts and it is a most useful manual. I may perhaps be allowed to quote his defence of the necessity of a knowledge of both the Civil and the Canon Law:

> For, *First*, if you take away this Law, we have no just Method and Form of Proceeding in Judicial Causes of an Ecclesiastical Cognizance; since this Form is only compriz'd and set down in the second Book of the *Decretals*. And, *Secondly*, We shall be without the Decisions of several important and considerable Controversies; which, being taken from the Laws of Nature and of Nations, are not to be met with in any other Books but in those of the *Civil* and *Canon-Law*. And *Thirdly*, The Lawyers themselves will be without the united Knowledge of both these Laws to their great Disadvantage: for as the Interpreters of the *Canon-Law* are deem'd but very unskilful Instructers without the Knowledge of the *Roman Civil-Law*; so are the Interpreters of the *Civil-Law* reckon'd but mean Lawyers with[2] a due and proper Understanding of the *Canon-Law*. And both these Laws are at this Day so link'd together, that no one can be said

[1] In addition to the *D.N.B.*, see *The Case of Dr Ayliffe at Oxford* (1716).
[2] Ayliffe clearly means "without".

to be a Lawyer beyond Sea, without understanding both of them: And he is entirely ignorant of both of these Laws, who contents himself with the Knowledge of one of these alone.[1]

The body of Ayliffe's work is arranged in alphabetical order, and he has three folio pages under the title *Of Custom, and of the Nature and Force thereof, etc.*[2] Here we have the pure canonical and civil law doctrine with references to the Decretals, the Digest, and the medieval commentators, and there is no suggestion whatever, either here or in his preface, that Ayliffe regards this part of the subject as obsolete.

These instances supply some authority in the jurisprudence of the post-Reformation English Church for the statements which I quoted earlier from the Canon Law Report. They are few because, as I have said, our reports of cases before the nineteenth century are fragmentary, and because the majority of cases in which custom was alleged concerned those matters of which the common law courts claimed cognizance. I suspect that a fuller investigation of the manuscript material surviving from the eighteenth and early nineteenth centuries might supply more instances than I have given here, and I hope that some day we may see in print a thorough examination of this subject.

Before leaving the point, however, I would like to draw your attention to its application in the field of public worship. The Book of Common Prayer is annexed to a statute, and its rubrics are generally regarded by the lawyers as statutory rules. This means that no variation from them can be allowed, no custom can affect them, they cannot lose their force. In 1811 the doctrine which was later affirmed by the Judicial Committee of the Privy Council was stated by Sir John Nicholl in the Court of Arches in a case brought by a Mr

[1] *Parergon*, pp. xxxvi f.
[2] Ibid. pp. (194)–(6). There are two sets of pages numbered 189–196, the numbers on the second set being in brackets.

Francis Newbery, of Heathfield, Sussex, against his vicar, Dr Goodwin.[1] It appears that the vicar was in the habit of leaving out parts of the lessons, and on a particular Sunday, after having omitted part of a verse of the first lesson, he looked round to Mr Newbery's pew and said: "I have been accused by some ill-natured neighbour of making alterations in the service; I have done so now, and shall do so again, whenever I think it necessary; therefore mark." Before examining the particulars of the case Sir John Nicholl laid down the following principles:

> The law directs that a clergyman is not to diminish in any respect, or to add to the prescribed form of worship;—uniformity in this respect, is one of the leading and distinguishing principles of the Church of England,—nothing is left to the discretion and fancy of the individual. If every minister were to alter, omit, or add according to his own taste, this uniformity would soon be destroyed, and though the alteration might begin with little things, yet it would soon extend itself to more important changes in the public worship of the Established Church, and even in the Scriptures themselves;—the most important passages might be materially altered, under the notion of giving a more correct version,—or omitted altogether, as unauthorized interpolations.[2]

Later in the century in the case of Martin *v.* Mackonochie the Privy Council declared a similar view:

> Their Lordships are of opinion that it is not open to a Minister of the Church, or even to their Lordships in advising her Majesty, as the highest Ecclesiastical Tribunal of Appeal, to draw a distinction in acts which are a departure from, or a violation of, the Rubric, between those which are important and those which appear to be trivial. The object of a Statute of Uniformity is, as its preamble expresses, to produce 'an universal agreement in the public worship of Almighty God', an object which would be wholly frustrated if each Minister,

<hr />

[1] I *Phillimore*, pp. 282–6.   [2] Ibid. pp. 282 f.

on his own view of the relative importance of the details of the Service, were to be at liberty to omit, to add to, or to alter any of those details.[1]

In a valuable Appendix to the 1906 Royal Commission on Ecclesiastical Discipline Bishop Gibson of Gloucester quoted this judgement, and then observed:

> But as a matter of history (1) at all periods practices not enjoined in, and omissions from the requirements of the rubrics have been common, being often not merely acquiesced in, but even approved and sanctioned by Episcopal authority; while (2) every attempt to enforce the strict letter of the law by coercive measures has proved disastrous, and led to a schism in the Church, "conscience" in each case being pleaded by the recalcitrant party.[2]

He proceeded to illustrate this by nine pages of examples.

In view of these dicta some interest attaches to a case which came before the Canterbury diocesan court in 1741 and was brought by the churchwardens of Chartham, Kent, against their rector, Mr Tilsley. Unhappily I have not been able to search for the official record of it in the act books of the court, but there are full notes of it among Sir George Lee's papers, and it is on these that I base my account.[3]

There were eight principal charges against Tilsley, which were these: (1) That he did not catechize the children regularly on Sundays and particularly on the Sundays during Lent, 1740. (2) That he refused to visit a Mrs Hockwell who was sick in September, 1739. (3) That he refused to christen the child of Simon Wood when it was brought to church on Sunday, 30 March 1740. (4) That he did not give

[1] W. G. Brooke, *Six Judgments of the Judicial Committee of the Privy Council in Ecclesiastical cases, 1850–1872*, London (1872), p. 119.

[2] *Report of the Royal Commission on Ecclesiastical Discipline*, London (1906), iv, pp. 49–57.

[3] MS. Eng. Misc. c. 31, ff. 135–42, *George and Cook agst. Tilsley*.

notice of Feast and fasting days and of administering the Sacrament, and this particularly with reference to Good Friday and Easter Day, 1740. (5) That he did not read the prayers in the afternoon on Christmas Day, 1739, nor on Good Friday, 1740, nor in the Ember week in Lent, 1740, nor on Wednesdays and Fridays in Lent, 1740. The notes about this charge are difficult to follow, and the omission to read the Litany on Wednesdays and Fridays seems to have become confused with the omission of Evensong at the other times. (6) That he neglected to read the collect appointed to be read in time of war when the country was at war with Spain. (7) That he refused to administer the sacrament at home to three people who were sick and desired to receive it, one of whom died without the sacrament. (8) That ever since 9 March 1740 he had forbidden the Clerk to give out a psalm after the sermon, "to the grief of those in the parish who delight in Psalmody".

Two of these charges were not established. It was not proved that the message asking him to visit Mrs Hockwell had in fact ever been delivered to Tilsley, and on the charge relating to the refusal to baptize he successfully pleaded that the child was brought late. The judgement on this point reads:

> The fact that he did refuse to Christen the child on that day is sufficiently proved, but I think such refusal was not criminal because the child was not brought in due time, the Rubrick directs that children shall be baptised immediately after the 2nd lesson at morning, or evening service and I conceive the Minister is not to keep the whole Congregation waiting while he reads the office of Baptism over and over again but the parishioners are to take care to be at the font with their children when the 2nd lesson is ended.[1]

On all the other points Tilsley was found to have offended.

> Sentence therefore (the judgment reads) must be given against him for the promoters and he must be decreed to be

[1] MS. Eng. Misc. c. 31, f. 141 v.

admonished for the future to Catechise children and ignorant persons every Sunday in the afternoon in Lent, to give notice in the Church according to the Rubrick for observing of feast and fasting days, and of administring the Sacrament, to read prayers on Christmas days morning and afternoon and on Good Fridays and on Wednesdays and Fridays in every Lent in the mornings, to read the Collect appointed to be read in time of war in the morning as well as in the evening service, to administer the Sacrament at home upon notice given him according to the Rubrick to such of his parishioners as are sick and unable to come to church and desire to receive it, to desist from restraining the Parish Clerk to give out a Psalm to be sung at such times as Psalms have been heretofore usually sung in the parish Church of Chartham.[1]

All of these charges save one concerned a failure to carry out some duty which the Prayer Book imposed or which was required by the canons. The last charge, however, cannot be included under this description, for there is no rule which requires that a psalm should be sung after the sermon and, if we go by Sir John Nicholl's dictum, such a psalm is an addition to the service, and therefore a violation of the principle of Uniformity. The truth of the matter seems to be that the singing of a psalm at this point was an established liturgical custom at Chartham, and when the incumbent tried to suppress it the court ordered him not to interfere with it. Such a protection of the parishioners against a tiresome parson is a particularly interesting example of the equitable spirit in which the ecclesiastical courts at this time tried to administer the law.

In these lectures we have been concerned almost entirely with the ecclesiastical law in England in the period before the great controversial doctrinal and ritual cases which occupied so much of the second half of the nineteenth century. At the very time when the church needed the services

---

[1] MS. Eng. Misc. c. 31, ff. 141 v., 142.

of a body of men bred up in the traditions of her own jurisprudence she was deprived of it.   Indeed, the process of
handing over this profession to those who were strictly
amateurs in it began in 1832 with the replacement of the
Delegates by the Privy Council.   In 1843, well before the
criticism of that body which followed the Gorham judgement of 1851, Sir Robert Phillimore had seen its fundamental weakness when he wrote:

> But it can scarcely be denied that the substitution of the
> Judicial Committee of the Privy Council for the Court of
> Delegates operated not only unfavourably but unjustly upon
> our profession. In the latter Court five civilians sat with three
> Common Law Judges in all cases of appeal; in the new tribunal
> it may and does sometimes happen that no civilian at all sits,
> but that four Judges from the Common Law or Chancery de-
> termine even upon points of *practice* in the Ecclesiastical courts.
> It would be a curious sight to behold four civilians sitting in
> judgment as Court of Appeal upon cases—especially cases of
> *practice*—from Westminster Hall and Lincoln's Inn; though it
> would be difficult to say why the injury done would be greater
> or the injustice more flagrant in the latter than the former case.[1]

I have listened to many arguments in support of the jurisdiction exercised by the Judicial Committee of the Privy
Council with regard to ecclesiastical cases, but I have heard
none which touches this point that the members of that body
need not have had and for the most part have not had any
training in the law which they are expected to administer in
such cases. If throughout the last century we had had a final
court of appeal whose members could not be criticized on
grounds of lack of acquaintance with the law that they administered, the history of our Church might have been much
happier, and her life more orderly at the present day.

A second source of weakness has been the great increase
of statutory legislation in ecclesiastical affairs. From the

[1] R. J. Phillimore, *The Study of the Civil and Canon Law*, p. 43.

Restoration of Charles II to the second half of the nineteenth century there was no legislation at all by canon, and yet during this time grave and far-reaching changes were made in the law and constitution of the English Church. From the point of view of institutions, though not of course of doctrine, the forty years between 1820 and 1860 wrought as great a revolution as the corresponding period in the sixteenth century, if not indeed greater. Yet in this nineteenth century change the constitutional assemblies of the church, the convocations, had no share. They had been suppressed in 1717. They were not allowed to meet again for business until the middle of the nineteenth century, but then their revival was regarded with great suspicion in some quarters, and by modern standards they were unrepresentative, containing only two elected proctors from each diocese. They produced a number of extremely valuable and learned reports, but they hardly became legislative bodies until the composition of the Lower Houses had been broadened in 1920. During this time of their abeyance the view had established itself that canons were concerned with a small and rarified area of the church's life and that statutory legislation was really the best modern way of doing things. This view was consecrated, so to speak, by the Enabling Act and the creation of the Church Assembly, which might not unfairly be described as existing for the purpose of promoting Parliamentary legislation. Whatever other merits it may have, a statute is not the best instrument for directing the spiritual life of a community, and that, I believe, the experience of the last hundred years has shown.

It is interesting to find how again this was apparent to Sir Robert Phillimore, writing in 1843, before the fiercest controversies had begun:

Perhaps (he said), if, during the last twenty years, the "Corpus Juris Canonici", and still more, if the Provincial Constitutions of our country, as given in Lyndewode, had been

75

more thoroughly known and more deeply studied, the Church might have escaped some of those impediments which have been thrown in the way of her discipline and development by Acts of Parliament, framed with the best intentions for the support of her interests. It is sad to think how often a deeper acquaintance with her jurisprudence would have prevented this hasty and crude legislation; how frequently the positive enactment of to-day has been found to mar the wisdom of her ancient law. I must think that she has often been forgetful or ignorant of the treasures of her own Code when she had recourse to Parliament, thereby parting with some of her dignity, and at the same time depriving herself of the possession of a flexible system of jurisprudence, based on great principles which, under the direction of prudence and firmness, might have been well adapted to her successive exigencies.[1]

The law of the church differs greatly from systems of secular law in the variety of its subject matter. At the one extreme it deals with the same kind of things as the secular law, property, revenues, and personal freedom, which so often depends upon economic security. With all these the temporal power is concerned, and it may be that the best way to regulate them is by statutory legislation. But the law of the church is also concerned with much more that is less tangible. It deals with the application of the divine law and the preservation of the principles of church life which are found in the Scriptures, with the selection and ordination of the ministry, the administration of the sacraments, the conduct of public worship, and the outward pattern of the devotional life. The aim of church law is to preserve, to direct, and to educate. It does not therefore consist primarily of a series of commands and prohibitions to which penalties are attached, though it contains some of this. Much of it is rather normative and exhortatory and when penalties are necessary its favourite instrument is admonition. Part of it is immutable

<hr>

[1] R. J. Phillimore, op. cit. pp. 52 f.

from its universally recognized connection with the divine revelation, but much of it needs to be adapted to the circumstances of ages, countries, and communities. That is why the greater part of church law cannot be comprehended in a written code, and why its constituent parts need to be subject to other less elaborate and final methods of modification than statutory enactment. The danger is of course that flexibility may lead to licence, to such a variety of practice and entrenchment of selfish and partisan interests as will damage the church. I believe that we shall do best to seek for protection against this danger in a proper system of courts staffed by the right kind of officers rather than in an elaboration of the details of the law.

The debates upon the present revision of the canons have so far been conducted with very great charity, an absence of partisanship, and a desire to reach agreement. At least that is so as far as the Convocations are concerned. Nevertheless it seems to me that there is an undercurrent of fear which occasionally breaks out into the open. Men of more than one tradition fear that the life of the church is going to be tied and shackled for generations by a written code of law whose every detail may be imposed by all the penalties at the disposal of the courts. The effect of this fear is seen in a multitude of amendments to particular canons, amendments designed to make a place in the written law for this or that local exception, or to safeguard beyond any question this or that party principle. In other words, the canons are treated as if they were clauses in a Church Assembly Measure and intended to become Acts of Parliament. How foreign all this is to the true spirit of ecclesiastical law will, I hope, be apparent from the history that we have been considering in these three lectures, but the collapse of the canonical tradition and the activities of the Church Assembly make it intelligible.

The Report of the Canon Law Commission observes that "the success of a new code of canons will to a great extent

F

depend on a wider knowledge than at present exists among the clergy of the law of the Church of England, its nature, history, development, and particular characteristics". It goes on to refer to a statement by Sir Lewis Dibdin that "since the disappearance of Doctors' Commons in 1857 there has really been no method of teaching or preserving a knowledge of the Ecclesiastical Law". The Report then says:

> It is impossible at this stage to revive anything like Doctors' Commons, but we would suggest that a society, consisting of clergy, professional historians, and lawyers, be formed for the purpose of studying the Ecclesiastical Law and of suggesting ways in which that law either needs alteration or can be developed to meet new needs. As a rule there is far too little contact and interchange of ideas and points of view between the clergy and ecclesiastical lawyers, and such a society would give opportunities for this. Such a society would train up a number of people competent to advise and help the clergy in the particular problems of Ecclesiastical Law with which from time to time they are confronted.[1]

This is, to my mind, one of the most important proposals in the whole Report, and yet it has been virtually ignored. I am not sure, however, that it goes far enough, for it is very timidly based on the voluntary principle of those who have time to spare and like this sort of thing. I believe that all our attempts at reform will be crippled unless we can ensure that from the final court of appeal downwards those who are to be judges of the law shall have had a thorough training in it, and by that I mean not merely an acquaintance with Church Assembly Measures and such dessicated textbooks as Cripps' *Law Concerning the Church and Clergy* and Halsbury's *Laws of England*, but a real grounding in canonical jurisprudence, which of course includes more than a rudimentary knowledge of theology.

[1] *The Canon Law of the Church of England*, p. 97.

This raises the problem of money, because the acquisition of such knowledge will take time, and I am certain that we shall not get enough trained men to establish a corporate tradition unless there is some financial inducement. I think that as a result of the ancient method of payment by fees it is hardly realized by the clergy and churchpeople at large what a deal of service is already rendered by our legal officers for a comparatively small reward. So long as the Church of England maintains contact with its past, and so long as it remains the Established Church of this country, the legal officers will be necessary to its proper functioning. Already it is difficult in some parts of the country to find men who have the necessary legal status and have any knowledge at all of ecclesiastical law, and in the opinion of those best able to judge, this difficulty is likely to grow. If we are to have church law at all—and I do not see how a church like ours can very well function without it—it is vital that we have properly trained and qualified lawyers. Unless there is some real financial inducement, and unless some test such as a Lambeth Diploma is instituted, I do not see how this is to be brought about. A society such as is proposed by the Canon Law Report can do something, but its effect will be long term and pervasive. It can be no adequate substitute for professional training and the provision of opportunities for such training ought to have much more attention that it has so far received.

One thing of particular value, however, such a society could do. It could bring lawyers and clergymen together and help each group to a greater understanding of the other's point of view. It could also encourage the study of the law of the church among the clergy. In these lectures no mention has been made of the clerical canonists who have played an important part in the history of the Church of England, bishops such as Gibson and Stillingfleet, priests such as Dr Richard Burn. In the eighteenth century and to some extent

79

in the nineteenth also there were clergymen with sufficient legal training to be chancellors of dioceses and to help in the formation of the ecclesiastical legal tradition. It is doubtful, however, whether an attempt to revive clerical chancellors is desirable. The clergymen who have an interest in the subject are perhaps better occupied in study, in teaching, and in advising than in the administration of the law. For certain types of case they would have to give place to a person trained in the rules of evidence, and it is perhaps better that they should not be involved at all. Moreover, it may be observed that the posts of chancellor and registrar provide at the very centre of the church's administration opportunities for laymen to contribute their special knowledge and ability and introduce a lay as distinct from a clerical element.[1] It is, however, important that clergymen and lawyers should understand one another, and such a society as has been proposed might help much to that end. It may be added that there is an important place for the Universities to fill in this scheme, and the recent appointment of the head of a Cambridge College to be Dean of the Arches is a hopeful sign.

The re-creation of something like the tradition of Doctors' Commons is, to my mind, the only really satisfactory answer to the fears which I mentioned, but it will be almost impossible to renew that tradition unless the ecclesiastical law can be freed from its entanglement with statute law as that has developed in the last century and a half. Such a suggestion is in no way intended as an attack on the Royal Supremacy. Canons are not a means of legislation which evades the control of that Supremacy. In England no canon becomes binding upon the clergy until it has received the royal assent, and the Queen can give her assent only on the advice of some minister who is answerable to Parliament for the advice

[1] This is, of course, always subject to the proviso that such lawyers should be well grounded in theology, particularly in the doctrines of the church and of the sacraments.

which he gives. We have, in fact, two parallel methods of legislation, one by Church Assembly Measure leading to an Act of Parliament, the other by canon. Both stand under the Royal Supremacy. The one leads to statute law, the other to canon law. Statute law is inflexible, canon law is flexible, and therefore canon law is more suitable for considerable parts of the church's life in which adaptability to circumstance is needed. In the current revision of the canon law there will be an opportunity to redress the balance as between statute and canon when it comes to deciding upon the steps necessary to give effect to those of the canons which alter the existing law. Church Assembly Measures and Acts of Parliament will be needed to do this, but it is important that they should be liberating and enabling acts, that they should free parts of the church's life to canonical jurisprudence and not bring more of it into the realm of statute law.

There is one more point which should be made in the light of recent debates upon the revision of the canons. It has from time to time been objected against certain of the proposals that they were exhortations and not law. Such an objection is based upon a grave misunderstanding of the nature of canon law. As has been indicated earlier in these lectures, that law has always consisted in part of explicit enactments to the transgression of which penalties were attached, but only in part. Much of the canon law has always been concerned with the norms of conduct, and has indicated standards which the church thought ought to be observed but was not prepared to enforce by action at law. In the canons of the early councils there are some to which anathemas are attached and others which have no such sanction. Among the canons of 1603 is one which speaks of the reverence and attention to be used within the church in time of divine service. Sir George Lee, in a judgement given in 1753, declined to allow an appeal based in part upon this canon, saying: "That the Canon of 1603, was exhortatory,

81

but did not inflict any penalty." [1] Undoubtedly there are parts of the law of the church which must be enforceable, if necessary by action in the courts, but to think of the whole of church law in those terms is a complete misconception and shows how far the modern Church of England has moved from its inheritance. That we may use the opportunity given by the current revision of the canons to recover that inheritance is the plea of these lectures. We seek freedom to develop again such a jurisprudence as will best serve the maintenance and edification of the Christian life among our people, a jurisprudence which our church once had and which the neglect of some and the ill-judged enthusiasm of others in the nineteenth century allowed to decay.

[1] I *Lee*, p. 436.

INDEX

ADAM of Usk, 33 f., 36
Admiralty, court of, 35, 37, 40 f., 43 f., 48, 51 f.
Alexander III, pope, 65
Ancharano, *see* Peter de
Andrew, Dr J., 62
Anthony de Butrio, canonist, 23
Aquinas, Thomas, O.P., 26
Arches, court of, 37 f.
    dean of the, 37, 40, 80. *See also* Beckington, Blodwell, Fust, Harvey, Lee, Lushington, Nicholl, Phillimore
Armagnac, count of, 35
Arundel, Thomas, abp. of Canterbury, 34
Athon *or* Ayton, *see* John of
Aylesbury, Buckinghamshire, 42
Ayliffe, Dr J., 67–69

Baisio, *see* Guido de
Baptism, 17, 58–60, 71–73
Beckington, Thomas, bp. of Bath and Wells, 35 f.
Bentham, Jeremy, 51
Beresford-Hope, A. J. B., 54
Bernard of Parma, canonist, 21
Bettesworth, Dr, advocate, 66
Beverley, *see* John of
Beyrouth, university of, 19
Blackstone, Sir William, 51
Blanche, princess, 34
Blodwell, Dr Richard, dean of the Arches, 36
Bodleian Library, Oxford, 42, 61 f.
Bologna, university of, 17, 21
Boniface, abp. of Canterbury, 27
Boniface VIII, pope, 12, 16, 18, 28. *See also* Sext
Book of Common Prayer, 58 f., 69–73
Bordeaux, 34
Boswell, James, 43

Bridgnorth, peculiar of, 40
Bristol, diocese of, 47
Bruges, 34
Brys, J., 26
Buckinghamshire, 41 f.
Burn, Dr Richard, 49, 51, 79
Butrio, *see* Anthony de

Calendar, 17
Calvinism, 45
Cambridge, university of, 37, 47. *See also* Trinity Hall.
Campbell, Lord, Lord Chancellor, 53
Canonization of saints, 30
Canon law, Report of archbishops' Commission on, 30 f., 63 f., 69, 77–79
Canons and Constitutions Ecclesiastical, 1603/4, v, 81 f.
Canterbury, abps. of, 12–14, 26, 51 f., 54. *See also* Arundel, Boniface, Chichele, Langton, Pecham, Sheldon, Tennison.
    convocation of, 34 f. *See also* Convocation
    courts of, 34, 38. *See also* Arches, Prerogative
    dean of, 39
    diocese of, 40, 71
    province of, 12 f., 31, 34, 38, 43
Carthage, council of, 24
Cathedrals, 32
Chancellor, Lord High, 52 f.
Chancellors, 49, 63, 79 f.
Chancery, court of, 39, 74
Chappuis, Jean, 17
Charles II, king, 39 f., 75
Chartham, Kent, charges against incumbent of, 71–73
Chichele, Henry, abp. of Canterbury, 27
Chivalry, court of, 34 f.

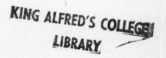